The Evolving Role of China
in International Institutions

Prepared for:

The U.S.-China Economic and Security Review Commission

Prepared by:

Stephen Olson
Clyde Prestowitz

The Economic Strategy Institute
3050 K St NW Suite 200
Washington DC, 20007

January 2011

TABLE OF CONTENTS

About the Economic Strategy Institute

The Economic Strategy Institute (ESI) is a private, non-profit, non-partisan public policy research organization dedicated to assuring that globalization works with market forces to achieve maximum benefits rather than distorting markets, and imposing costs. This should be achieved on the basis of principles, policies, and institutions consistent with democratic values. Because security and national welfare will increasingly depend on performance in the global marketplace, the Economic Strategy Institute is particularly concerned with developing national and corporate strategies to assure that globalization takes place on a level playing field and the reality is mutually beneficial.

The Institute is a firm believer in markets, but it knows that all markets operate within boundaries of different rules and institutions. ESI studies and understands the importance of macroeconomic factors such as interest rates, exchange rates, and savings rates. But, unlike many economic policy organizations, ***ESI places particular emphasis on institutional and structural factors and on the circumstances of the particular industries that make up the overall economy***. It is, after all, impossible to have a smoothly running machine if the key components are faulty. Accordingly, ESI analyzes major industries and technologies as well as domestic and international economic industrial policies.

The growing importance of globalization and ESI's practical, business-like approach to the issues have made the institute a major player in government circles since its founding in 1989. ESI's staff shape opinion and strategy by publishing books, articles and editorials as well as by providing testimony to Congress and private consultation to government and business leaders. The institute also conducts a number of influential conferences and lectures throughout the year.

Over the past decade, ESI has had a major influence on the conclusion of the NAFTA and Uruguay Round negotiations, U.S. economic and trade policy towards Japan, China and Europe, and telecommunications, international aviation, and other important economic and trade issues. ESI has also helped shape strategy for a number of multinational corporations.

As we move into the next century, the world's marketplace will become even more complex to corporations, governments, and consumers. The Economic Strategy Institute is well suited to tackle these complexities and provide expert analyses and leadership on the important elements of the globalized economy. As technology has shrunk time and distance over the past forty years, integration of the world's major markets into one global economy has proceeded at an increasingly rapid pace. This trend was greatly accelerated when the end of the Cold War opened virtually the entire world to the dynamism of capitalistic market forces.

Globalization is both necessary and desirable as rising costs of research and investment compel exploitation of worldwide markets and as nations realize that ***being left out means being left behind***. But precisely because globalization is inevitable, the terms on which it is accomplished are of critical importance. Globalization based on fair and transparent rules, mutually open markets, equal treatment of investors regardless of nationality, and competitive business practices is different from globalization based on mercantilism, cartels, administrative guidance, and unchecked speculation.

Introduction

The U.S.-China Economic and Security Review Commission ("the Commission") was established by Congress in 2000 to monitor and report to Congress on the economic and national security dimensions of the United States' trade and economic ties to the People's Republic of China ("PRC").

One of the primary arenas in which the evolving nature of the U.S.-China strategic and economic relationship has played out has been in the various international and regional institutions in which one or both countries participate, as well as the bilateral or multilateral economic partnerships and relationships which each country maintains. The growing influence of China has been felt across the board on all of these stages, and this study is aimed at understanding the full implications of this growing influence.

The study covers a number of issues and questions surrounding China's participation in international and regional institutions and forums. These issues and questions address the following broad themes:

1) What is China's posture, objectives and strategies within key international institutions, and in the context of its economic partnerships?

2) What are the trends, and the likely future trends over the next 5-10 years?

3) What are the implications for the United States, and what strategies should the United States pursue?

Summary of Key Findings

China's role and influence within a variety of international organizations is in the midst of an important evolution, which will have profound impacts on the manner in which the US pursues its international economic and strategic interests, both within and beyond the surveyed institutions.

China has demonstrated an increasingly assertive and proactive stance within these organizations, which has combined in some cases with greater institutional power. Across the board, China has become more effective in utilizing international organizations to advance national interests, and to extract what it needs from these institutions. China's growing role not only supports its strategic interests, but, it should be acknowledged, is also frequently constructive and helpful for the organizations in which it participates. Furthermore, to the extent these organizations accomplish work that is beneficial to the global community at large, China rightfully deserves its fair share of credit for its support and contributions. Importantly, from a tactical point of view, China's constructive engagement in these organizations is shrewd because it heightens Chinese credibility, which further strengthens China's influence, and its ability to achieve its objectives.

While a number of factors have contributed to China's growing influence, the Global Financial Crisis (GFC) warrants special attention, acting as an accelerant which deepened and hastened an evolution that was already underway. Although the basic parameters of the GFC are well known, a quick review of some of the key points will help illuminate the "hows and whys" of China's strengthened position within international institutions.

The United States is emerging from the GFC in a weakened economic condition, saddled with a debilitating level of debt, persistently high unemployment, and anemic growth rates. Perhaps of equal if not greater importance is the reputational damage that has been done to the philosophical pillars upon which the U.S. model of capitalism has been built: the primacy of the marketplace, a light government hand, free and open trade and investment policies, and a public and private mentality of borrow and spend, borrow and spend, borrow and spend.

China meanwhile, is emerging from the GFC in a stronger relative economic position, having just overtaken Japan as the second largest economy in the world. While the United States and much of Europe were plunged into the steepest recession in 80 years, China plowed through the crisis with hardly a dip in its remarkable rates of growth. Of potentially greater long-term importance is the fact that the fallout from the GFC has, especially in the eyes of many in the developing world, bolstered the credibility of China's economic development model, and fed a growing sense that while the 20th Century was the American Century, the 21st Century might just be China's.

As the United States is wrestling with a debt burden that will likely start imposing at least some limitations on spending and borrowing, China is sitting on top of the largest foreign currency reserves in the world – and they are growing.[1] China has an increasing capacity (both financial and philosophical) to project itself onto the world stage. Although still far behind that of the United States, Chinese military capacity – especially its desire to create a blue water navy -- is steadily increasing. On the U.S. side, two lengthy wars have taken a heavy toll, and new budgetary realities have forced Defense Department officials to focus more and more of their attention on where and how to cut, rather than how to grow.

China's foreign currency reserves also puts in it in a position to provide significant levels of development aid and assistance, and the size of its market, along with a rapidly growing middle class, means that access to the Chinese market will be increasingly important for the balance sheet of companies not just in Asia, but elsewhere in the world as well. To take but one example, China has already become the largest market for automobiles in the world, but in relative terms, only a small percentage of the population have cars, meaning that the size of that market could continue to grow by leaps and bounds. Similar dynamics exist in a range of other important consumer segments.[2]

---

[1] Mc Gregor, Richard. "China's unbalanced economy", Financial Times, May 21, 2007;

[2] Anderlini Jamil and Mure Dikie, "China A Future on track", Financial Times, September 23, 2010;

In the decades since China gradually began opening its economy, and adopting market-based reforms, it has clearly played the role of "student," learning from Western-style market capitalism, and from the United States in particular. U.S. officials, in consultations and negotiations with their Chinese counterparts, oftentimes felt comfortable in delivering what could be described as "lectures" on how the Chinese economy should be managed. And while Chinese leaders never envisioned or desired a world in which China would fully replicate the America capitalist system, there was undeniably a recognition that there was much to learn to from the US and Western European economic models, especially the deep and mature capital markets, and the effective regulatory regimes overseeing the financial system.

Today – it goes without saying -- we are living in a much changed world. The days in which China is viewed as an economic "student" are probably gone forever. As one Chinese official wryly observed: "The teachers seem to have made a few mistakes."[3]

In short, China has become:

1) An increasingly important trade and investment partner, in many instances displacing the United States as the largest trading partner for countries not only in Asia, but in other regions as well.

2) An increasingly important source of aid and development assistance.

3) An increasingly relevant and attractive model of economic development.

<u>What does all this mean?</u>

China and International Institutions

China's remarkable growth story, and its strengthened relative position as result of the GFC, cannot help but deeply impact the make-up and functioning of the international institutions in which it participates, many of which have traditionally mirrored a US view of the world. In the aftermath of the economic crisis, China's calls for greater representation in institutions such as the World Bank and the International Monetary Fund became more vociferous, and other nations, including western developed nations, have seemed to signal a greater receptivity to this notion. The moral authority and credibility the Chinese can now carry into a variety of international economic institutions is greater than it ever has been.

In the aftermath of the Second World War and the Great Depression, the United States was in a position to stamp its philosophical imprint on a panoply of multilateral institutions, ranging from the United

---

[3] Wolf, Martin. "Wheel of Fortune Turns as China Outdoes West." Financial Times, September 14, 2009.

Nations, the World Bank, the IMF, and the WTO predecessor organization, the General Agreement on Tariffs and Trade (GATT). In subsequent decades, as additional international or regional organizations came into being, the US continued to be highly effective in ensuring these newer additions also reflected to a large extent the same underlying philosophies.

We have now, however, likely entered the beginning of the end of this chapter. In the years and decades to come, organizations will evolve differently, and in some respects, away from the U.S.-influenced philosophical foundations upon which they were built. Institutional policies and governance structures will gradually shift to reflect the priorities, needs, and interests of a wider range of countries. New organizations, built upon a different set of assumptions and philosophies, will come into being, and in some instances, challenge the relevance of their predecessors.

China did not have a seat at the table when the rules were written for the first-generation international institutions. But China has seat at the table today, and it's getting bigger. It will use its rising influence to shape, to the extent it can, the rules of the game. China has shown a seriousness of purpose in its approach to international institutions, and has learned to "play the game" well. While the United States was the driving force behind the establishment of the post-War international institutional architecture, China might ultimately prove to be a more adept navigator of the terrain. Of potentially even greater impact is China's ability to shift influence towards new institutions that might not necessarily be grounded in the same philosophical underpinnings.

But whether we look at long-standing organizations or newly emerging institutions and groupings, China's influence will cause these bodies to evolve in ways that are not always helpful for U.S. interests.

<u>Ten Trends and Two Truisms</u>

Broadly speaking, ten major trends and two truisms are identifiable in the evolution of China's participation in the institutions and organizations under review. These trend lines emerge from the public record, policy documents, statements, and transcripts, and from interviews and off-the-record conversations with officials and long-time observers actively engaged in these organizations over a period of time. These longtime participants and observers have had in effect a "front row" seat from which to observe China's evolution over the years, throughout countless hours spent in official consultations, working groups, and board meetings within the organizations in which they serve. It is from these first-hand experiences that some of the most striking illustrations of China's evolution emerge.

Given that the organizations under review are fairly diverse, not all of these trends are equally relevant in each organization. They do however apply across the board, to one degree or another, from organization to organization. The nuances and distinctions between and within specific organizations will be fully elucidated in the sections devoted to each organization.

The ten trends and two truisms are:

1. Greater Assertiveness, Greater Maturity

By all accounts and by any measure, China has demonstrated a steadily increasing activism and assertiveness in international organizations in recent years. This reflects China's growing economic might, as the country has continued its historically unprecedented charge up the economic development ladder. This growing assertiveness can be measured on several levels: in its ability to shape policies and positions within organizations, in its ability to use these organizations as platforms to project both hard and soft power, and in its ability to promote national interests. It is also noteworthy to point out that China has grown remarkably direct, and in some instances, almost confrontational in articulating its positions. If China ever felt the need to blunt its criticisms or soften its words, those days are clearly gone. For example, as will be further explored in the relevant sections below, China has been extremely pointed -- even strident -- in using IMF forums to blast what it views as the weaknesses and errors of U.S. economic and financial policy makers, while at the same time highlighting the positive global impact of Chinese policies.[4]

2. Expanding Influence

China's ability to influence institutions has grown steadily over the last 5-10 years, and has spiked even higher in the aftermath of the global financial crisis. This growing influence is visible across a spectrum of issues, ranging for the institutional culture within organizations to substantive issues of policy.

One way to define "influence" would be to characterize it as the ability to have your interests automatically factored into the decision-making of others, irrespective of whether you directly intervene yourself. "Influence" means that your interests and sensitivities have in effect become programmed onto the "hard drive" of others. And if we take this as a working definition of influence, then we can say emphatically that Chinese influence in regional and international institutions has grown dramatically in recent years. Whether it is an arcane procedural issue being discussed in a regional organization, or a critical geo-strategic issue being debated, there is an increasing sensitivity within institutions to the question: "What will China think?" China "casts a large shadow" within the organizations it participates

---

[4] See, for example: Statement by Dr. ZHOU Xiaochuan Governor of the People's Bank of China at the Twenty-First Meeting of the International Monetary and Financial Committee Washington D.C., April 24, 2010 http://www.cbrc.gov.cn/english/home/jsp/docView.jsp?docID=201010127105895E82201

in, and is able to wield influence directly and indirectly, in a variety of subtle, and not so subtle ways. For instance, as will be more fully described in the case study which follows, China uses the esoteric issue of organizational nomenclature to expand its influence and to establish a heightened sensitivity to Chinese concerns.[5] Although not always fully comprehended or appreciated from a Western perspective, these seemingly small "power plays" take on a much greater importance in the Asian context.

3. Broadening Sphere of Engagement

In recent years, China has shown an increasing tendency to project itself into a much wider range of issues within organizations, no longer restricting its attention to issues of direct impact on China. China has demonstrated a greater proclivity to become involved in administrative, procedural, or other "organizational" issues within the institutions they participate in. Now, and for the foreseeable future, China will play a much a greater role on a broader range of institutional and organization issues, and will seek to influence the operations and underlying architecture of these bodies.

For example, within APEC, China has become much more focused on reviewing and commenting on specific staff positions, and within the Asian Development Bank, China has begun delving much more deeply into proposed projects not related to China (see relevant sections below). As China broadens its engagement into issues such as these, it will have a greater ability to impact the way these institutions "look and feel" and operate.

4. Extreme Effectiveness

By any objective measure or criteria, China has evolved into a highly effective player in the organizations reviewed. Both in terms of its ability to advance its own agenda, as well as its ability to deflect objectionable proposals from other quarters, China is a shrewd, savvy, and successful operator. Examples of China's diplomatic effectiveness abound, and will be further described below, but some noteworthy examples include China's ability to shift the G-20 agenda away from issues it prefers not to discuss, and the negotiating skill it brought to bear in ensuring an outcome to the Copenhagen Climate Summit almost entirely in line with its objectives.[6]

A large part of this effectiveness flows from the high quality individuals and officials that China sends to participate in these institutions. Given the nature of "how business gets done" in international organizations, the effectiveness of a member country often correlates closely with the quality of the

---

[5] Interview with long-time ADB observer.

[6] Garnaut, John. "Don't Push US, China Warns Rich Countries". Sydney Morning Herald, January 11, 2010.

individuals it sends as representatives or delegates. China has, in recent years, chosen to send its best and brightest -- extremely smart, capable, articulate, and frequently Western-educated individuals to represent its interests. China has clearly made a strategic decision to bring its "A-team" to the work of international organizations, and this strategy is paying off.

5. Content to Play a "Defensive Game" (in *Some* Organizations)

There are institutions (APEC, for example), in which China is an active participant not out of desire to proactively achieve particular objectives or to support the institutional mission, but rather to monitor the agenda and to deflect (when need be) proposals or initiatives that it finds objectionable. In this sense, activism and participation does not necessarily denote support, and in fact can sometimes signal the exact opposite.

In these cases, China is like a soccer team that can be content with a nil-nil draw. It does not need to put the ball in the back of the net in order to win -- it can simply deflect the ball out of bounds, do a lot of passing, and take time off the clock. It can be difficult to overcome this defensive strategy, especially when you need to score in order to win – a position in which the United States frequently finds itself.

As will be described more fully in the relevant section below, China would have ambivalent feelings about APEC ever becoming a forceful and powerful vehicle for fostering trade and investment cohesion with the Asia Pacific. Given the prominent role the US plays in APEC, China would much prefer to see an alternative structure (one which does *not* include the United States) play this role. Therefore, within APEC, China can be content to play a defensive game on issues or agenda items which advance the APEC role on trade and investment, thereby "taking time off the clock" while institutions like ASEAN + 3 have an opportunity to solidify their position and role.

6. Greater Engagement: a Two-Way Street

As previously described, the most pronounced trend which emerges from an analysis of China's conduct in international organizations is a steady increase in China's engagement and influence. However, it would be a mistake to presume that this engagement is strictly a "one way street", in which China is becoming increasingly able to shape and mold institutions. As China becomes more integrated into the system of international institutions, there are some respects in which the policies and practices of the institution are able to impact – at least in small ways -- the way China operates. To be clear, international institutions have not and will not cause any bold or dramatic policy shifts in China, but some modest examples do exist of China moving towards practices which reflect the operating ethos of the organizations in which it participates.

China's growing involvement in the Asia Development Bank, for example, has gradually led to a higher comfort level with greater transparency in the loan process, and the protracted negotiations surrounding the opening of an ADB office in Beijing in the late 1990s resulted in some positive movement on issues like confidentiality of ADB documents. And within its activities under the umbrella of the United Nations, China has shown an increasing comfort level interacting with international civil society organizations, something which would have been unimaginable 10 or 15 years ago.

7. An Impressive Ability to Learn

China has a voracious appetite for squeezing every drop of useful knowledge, expertise and technical know-how it can out of the institutions in which it participates. In several institutions, China has become the leading member nation in requesting and consuming studies and policy analysis on a range of issues. Although China (as with any other country) has ministries full of capable staffers also conducting analysis on the same issues, China sees the value in also generating an independent viewpoint. This allows it to tap into, and profit from, the collective international expertise in these organizations. In more than one institution, the greatest demand for document translation is into Chinese. There is a running joke among longtime staff members of an Asian regional organization which speaks to this point. When staff members are unable to locate one of their own official institutional reports or studies in their files or archives, according to the joke, they should ask the Chinese, because they will surely have it.

China also taps heavily into the institutional networks for information sharing, and exchanges of best practices and technical expertise on economic issues (within APEC on food safety, for example), and UN peacekeeping operations provide the Chinese military with an opportunity to train with, and learn from, more technologically sophisticated forces. Throughout all the institutions in which it participates, China has demonstrated an impressive ability to learn.

8. An Increasingly Valuable and Constructive Participant – in at Least Some Respects

First, a caveat: there are those who would strongly object to this characterization, and would furnish example after example which would purport to demonstrate the oftentimes counterproductive conduct of China within a given international institution. In at least some instances, these objections would have merit. However, this does not negate the fact that China frequently and increasingly plays a constructive role within the institutions it participates.

China is thorough, exceedingly well-prepared and well organized about executing its responsibilities as an institutional member. It does its "homework" and raises detailed, substantive questions about matters which not only affect China's interests, but also on issues of purely institutional relevance. This includes questions about operational issues and structures, staffing and office locations, and a range of administrative issues.

For example, China has made constructive contributions to UN peacekeeping operations (as will be explored in detail below), and its increasing financial support for different organizations it participates in should also be acknowledged. [7]

In this sense, and notwithstanding any examples of obstructionism, China is in fact a solid and constructive member of many of the institutions in which it participates. And perhaps most importantly in terms of the scope of this study, China's constructive engagement is tactically wise because it enhances its capability to influence these institutions.

9. Ambivalence

Despite China's growing role in international institutions, there is nonetheless a contradictory impulse at the heart of the Chinese approach. A core tenant of China's political philosophy and foreign policy is the absolutely paramount supremacy of national sovereignty and the principle of non-involvement in the "internal affairs" of sovereign nations. Therefore, there will frequently be tension between this impulse, and the tug of international organizations, which pulls countries towards cooperative joint endeavors which rely on greater transparency and openness – and sometimes involvement in each other's "affairs."

For instance, UN peacekeeping operations are one forum in particular in which this tension comes to the forefront. Interestingly though, this is an area in which there has been an evolution in the Chinese viewpoint, and the PRC has shown greater pragmatism in supporting peacekeeping operations (see relevant chapter).

China long ago reached a firm decision that it needs to be an active player in international institutions. But due to the contradictory impulses at the heart of its political philosophy, it will always approach its participation in these institutions with a certain degree of ambivalence.

10. The Primacy of Taiwan

This is perhaps the most obvious of the ten trends: China utilizes its participation in international institutions, as well as its bilateral and regional relationships, to relentlessly promote the sanctity of the "One China" policy. In bilateral relationships, this is often transactional in nature. Developing countries that adhere to the One China policy are often recipients of Chinese aid programs and other forms of development assistance. In the context of international institutions, those countries that do not adhere to the One China policy will find Chinese opposition at every turn. In the Asian Development Bank, for

---

[7] International, Crisis Group, "China's Growing Role in UN Peacekeeping", Asia Report No. 166, April 17, 2009.

example, China votes against every project for the Solomon Islands. The Solomon Islands continues to be on the diminishing list of countries which recognize Taiwan. [8]

Finally, in addition to these ten trends, there are two truisms which much be borne in mind when reviewing China's role in specific institutions:

1. China's Greatest Objective is STABILITY.

Although the specifics of China's approach can vary from institution to institution, the one over-arching objective which informs and drives its conduct is the need for stability. Chinese leaders need – above all else – to ensure the existence of a benign and conducive global environment for China to continue to grow economically at a fast but sustainable pace -- in short, to continue its "peaceful rise."

As the US and other leading western developed countries continue to struggle with anemic growth rates, it would be understandable if US economic officials envied how "easy" life must be for their Chinese counterparts, as China's economy continues to steam along at growth rates approaching 10 percent. But such a view would represent a fundamental misunderstanding.

Much of the governing legitimacy of the Chinese Communist Party is derived from its ability to engineer the greatest economic growth story in recorded history, lifting hundreds of millions of Chinese citizens out of poverty, and creating a middle class with progressively expanding expectations. Given China's sheer size, and the significant development challenges it continues to face, China's growth rates are, in a sense, not astronomical at all. In fact, they are only slightly above the minimum levels which are required in order to continue to propel the China growth story, maintain employment, provide the standard of living that is increasingly expected, and continue to maintain the CCP's governing legitimacy.

The simple fact of the matter is this: a 6 percent growth rate in China would be an exponentially greater problem than a 2 percent growth rate in the United States. Should Chinese policy makers stumble, and fail to deliver the required growth, the societal and political impacts could be severe. Chinese society and culture is undergoing a profound and probably irreversible shift. An increasingly large swath of the China's citizens believe that "their time is now," and that tomorrow must be and will be better than today. The amount of pressure this places on the Chinese leadership to continue to deliver jobs, prosperity, and higher standards of living is intense.

Above all else, as we examine China's role and objectives in international institutions, is the need for stability – a stable global environment in which China can successfully pursue the very high growth rates

---

[8] *Website of Embassy of the Republic of China (Taiwan) in Solomon Islands. Http://www.taiwanembassy.org/SB*

that it absolutely requires. This prism, more than any other single consideration, will inform and explain China conduct in international institutions, and will help policy makers accurately anticipate future Chinese conduct.

2. International Organizations Do Not *Create* the Prevailing World Economic or Strategic Order – They *Reflect* the Prevailing World Order.

The world is changing. Institutions will either evolve to reflect the reality of the world in which they operate, or they will gradually drift toward irrelevance. Not long ago, the G-8 was one of, if not **the** most important institutions on the global stage. Today, it has been supplanted and largely subsumed by the G-20. China's growing economic and strategic might was one of the driving forces behind this dramatic shift in the G-8/G-20 constellation, and it would be naïve and unrealistic to think that the G-8/G-20 will be the only institutions profoundly impacted by China's rise.

Methodology and Contents

In examining the questions posed by this study, a number of relevant aspects were reviewed. However, China's real ability to influence these organizations has flowed from the increasing sophistication with which China "works" the system, and from the increasing heft China can command as a result of its extraordinary economic growth, and the fall-out from the Global Financial Crisis. These are the issues that will reveal the most about the questions under consideration, and they will therefore constitute the primary focus of this study.

It goes without saying that some institutions and organizations wield greater global impact and influence than others. The International Monetary Fund, for instance, exerts a considerably greater global influence on the financial system than does the Bank for International Settlements.

The variation in the relative impact of the organization under review is reflected in the depth of the treatment provided to each. Simply put, some sections are more detailed than others, as a function of the varying levels of importance. However, even for those institutions (primarily towards the end of the study) which warrant relatively lighter treatment, there are still important trends which can be discerned and lessons which can be learned. And at a minimum, emerging issues within these institutions should be flagged for further monitoring.

Interspersed throughout the text will be a number of brief "case studies." These case studies will highlight a particular issue in order to give some "real world" flavor to the broader themes discussed in the chapters. Finally, the study will conclude with a series of recommendations on how U.S. policy makers can best cope with China's evolving role and influence in international organizations.

CASE STUDY:

The Arcane World of Nomenclature

It is instructive to spend a few minutes considering a seemingly arcane procedural issue which nonetheless illustrates larger and more profound themes. Within any international organization in which China participates the seemingly innocuous question of nomenclature takes on a dramatically deeper meaning.

From the Chinese perspective, extreme sensitivities exist around the status of Taiwan. As such, China insists on a very precise nomenclature that must be employed when referencing this jurisdiction within the organizations in which it participates.

In the APEC context, the terminology which must be employed is "Chinese Taipei". In the ADB context, the term of art is "Taipei,China".[9] Do not think that there is a typographical error in this report, in that there is no space between Taipei and China. Although in standard English there should be a space between "Taipei," and "China", within the ADB, the space is forbidden. There is an interesting organizational folklore in the ADB as to the exact origin of this formulation (some claim it goes back to an error made by a typist during pre-word processing days that was never corrected), but whatever the history might be, it is now firmly entrenched as formal policy, and serves as a somewhat amusing metaphor for China's desire to ensure that there is no "space" – literal or figurative – between Taiwan and China.

Although seemingly amusing on the surface, these issues are regarded with deadly seriousness within the organizations. Any infraction of the established nomenclature will result in a swift and official rebuke.

Any person who has participated in the deliberations of international organizations with China can undoubtedly describe the palpable tension which is created when one delegate makes the mistake of referring to "Taiwan" rather than by the officially approved nomenclature within that organization. First of all, the room will be quite enough to hear a pin drop. Then there where will be a strong and immediate request by the Chinese representative for a "correction" to the record. Anyone who makes such a mistake once is unlikely to make it twice. In fact, at Board meetings within the Asian Development Bank, if a

---

[9] Interview with senior, long time ADB observer;

delegate does make an erroneous reference to "Taiwan", the meeting must be formally stopped, and an official statement clarifying the exact political status of "Taiwan" is read out. Only when this formal clarification and correction is complete can the Board meeting recommence.

Among staff members of international or regional organizations, there are frequently shared "war stories" about memos or emails which were circulated to members with an erroneous reference to "Taiwan." Staffers swap experiences about how quickly they received a strongly worded and officious response from the China representative, pointing out the "error" and insisting on a prompt retraction and correction.

While it would be easy to dismiss all of this as institutional quirkiness, there is actually a meaningful issue involved. China has successfully inculcated an extreme sensitivity within these organizations to Chinese sensibilities and viewpoints. Representatives to, and staff members at, these institutions are very rapidly "trained" and any deviations are very poorly regarded.

The same issues also arise in the NGOs in which China participates, such as the Pacific Basin Economic Council, and the Pacific Economic Cooperation Council, suggesting a comprehensive and methodical approach on the part of China.

Irrespective of whether or not it is intentional, China is able to "cast a long shadow" in these organizations, and to create the habit amongst participants of being acutely aware of Chinese sensitivities and positions. In subtle but yet meaningful ways, China's influence and ability to impact these organizations is heightened.

IMF AND THE WORLD BANK

Summary of Key Findings

When one looks at China's role and influence within (and on) international financial institutions, the following six realities become clear:

1) The credibility of the underlying doctrines, prescriptions, and governance of multilateral institutions has been battered in recent years. This has given rise to a scramble within some institutions to adapt policies, practices, and structures to bring them more in line with new global realities. In many instances, the most important "new global reality" these institutions must adjust to is China.

2) China's ability to influence and potentially shift the policies and practices of multilateral development institutions is growing, although institutional impediments to preponderant Chinese influence are still formidable.

3) The competence and efficacy of multilateral institutions in delivering aid is being increasingly questioned.

4) China has a growing financial capability to provide aid and loans in the developing world on a bilateral basis.

5) China's model of development assistance – no conditionality, plus lightning-quick speed and competency in execution – is favorably viewed in many quarters throughout the developing world, and stands in sharp contrast to the ambivalence with which many World Bank or IMF programs are viewed.

6) While its overall aid budget is still less than what the large institutions can provide, China is increasingly in a position to displace multilateral organizations as a source of development aid. China's aid program in Africa, for example, has already exceeded that of the World Bank.[10]

---

[10] Alden, Chris. "China and Africa's Natural Resources: The Challenges and Implications for Development and Governance." September 2009, South African Institute of International Affairs.

Philosophical Underpinnings

The Western/IMF/World Bank model imposes varying degrees of "conditionality" on recipient nations, on a wide range of issues involving the rule of law, accounting standards, transparency, and the development of civil society. Human rights practices do come under scrutiny, and the internal domestic practices of a particular country are viewed as very much the business of multilateral development institutions.

From an economic point of view, and particularly in the case of the IMF, the provision of funding has traditionally been contingent on certain macro-economic policy reforms that have reflected the prevailing Western economic wisdom and doctrine. [11]

These policy prescriptions largely derive from the so-called Washington Consensus, which essentially describes a number of market-based policy prescriptions that should form the basis for reform packages to be provided to developing countries experiencing acute economic difficulties.[12]

China's approach to its bilateral assistance programs is markedly different. There are no conditions imposed, and perhaps most importantly, the notion of "non-involvement" in a recipient country's "internal affairs" is firmly and implacably entrenched. This *laissez faire* attitude towards the domestic conduct of recipient governments has lead to international criticisms of China for providing assistance to a number of regimes (principally in Africa and Southeast Asia) with questionable human rights practices, in exchange for access to the commodities and raw materials needed to power China's continued growth. [13]

The Lingering Impact of the Asian Financial Crisis

An important watershed in the IMF's history took place during the Asian Financial Crisis of 1997. A number of countries in the region found themselves in dire economic straits and turned to the IMF for assistance. Unfortunately, the macro-economic policy prescriptions – derived from the principles of the Washington Consensus -- insisted upon by the IMF as a condition for the aid inflicted tremendous short term pain in many instances.[14] One country – Malaysia – struck a defiant tone, turned down IMF assistance and pursued a policy course largely at odds with the IMF prescriptions, particularly in regards

---

[11] Halper, Stefan. The Beijing Consensus: How China's Authoritarian Model Will Dominate The Twenty-First Century. New York: Basic Books, 2010. Page 58.

[12] Ibid, page 52

[13] Abdoulaye Wade, Senegal's President, "Time for the west to practice what it preaches", Financial Times, January 23,2008, http://www.ft.com/cms/s/5d347f88-c897-11dc-94a6-0000779fd2ac,dwp_uuid=8735dcb2

[14] Mark Weisbrot,"Standing up to the I.M.F", International Herald Tribune, Oct 7 2010.

to capital controls.[15] This bold move seemed to be vindicated by Malaysia's relative success in weathering the crisis, particularly in comparison with the experiences of some of its neighbors which did in fact sign on to the IMF program.

In the years following the Asian Financial crisis, in which many of the draconian policies required by the IMF generated widespread human suffering (and which directly or indirectly contributed to the toppling of at least one ruler), the term "conditionality" took on a pejorative tone in much of Asia.[16]

It is commonly said that a picture is worth a thousand words. There is no better example of this than a photograph taken at the height of the Asian Financial Crisis, and which appeared on the front page of newspapers around the world. It is a photograph taken at the signing ceremony on an aid package between the IMF and Indonesia.[17] The IMF Managing Director, Michel Camdessus, is standing above Indonesian President Suharto as he signs the agreement which included a number of painful policy reforms. Camdessus comes off as a stern school teacher, literally and figuratively looking down on Suharto, who seems to come off as a poorly performing student being reprimanded. This image is seared into the minds of many in Asia, and was reminiscent of painful colonial histories in many countries, in which European powers attempted to impose their way of doing things on Asian nations where these norms were not applicable or appropriate. This fed a growing perception that Western economic policy prescriptions – as dispensed by Western-dominated institutions -- were not always right for Asia, and in fact could sometimes be disastrous.[18] This seminal experience gave rise to a new mindset in which Asian alternatives were more eagerly sought and embraced, while the traditional Western medicine was viewed with increasing skepticism.

---

[15] Jacques, Martin. "Chinese in Top Job at World Bank". China Daily, March 6, 2008.

[16] Halper, page 59.

[17] Greenlees, Donald, "The Search for a New Financial Order", Global Asia, December 2008.

[18] Mark Weisbrot,"Standing up to the I.M.F", International Herald Tribune, Oct 7 2010.

As the IMF now finds itself with a new crisis to confront – this one Western in origin --It is interesting to note that we are currently witnessing a concerted and focused effort by the IMF to attempt to undo some of the unfortunate legacy of the Asian Financial crisis, and to re-orient itself to the sensibilities and priorities of Asia.

In what has been described as a "charm offensive" or a "mea culpa" tour , IMF managing director Dominque Strauss-Kahn has in recent months attempted to woo Asian audiences by signaling a recognition of the greater role of Asia both in the global economy and the IMF, and by candidly acknowledging previous IMF missteps in the region. [19]

Speaking recently in Korea, Strauss-Kahn plainly stated: "let me be candid: we have made some mistakes … Asia's time has come in the global economy, and so it must be at the IMF. Rapid growth has turned the region into a global economic powerhouse—and Asia's economic weight in the world is on track to grow even larger. This has been accompanied, quite rightly, by Asia's increasing importance—and influence—in global policy debates."[20]

---

[19] Dominique Strauss-Kahn, Managing Director of the IMF Opening Remarks at the Asia 21 Conference-Daejeon, "Asia and the Global Economy: Leading the way Forward in the 21st Century", Korea, July 12, 2010;

[20] Ibid.

Strauss-Kahn went even further, implicitly recognizing a shift in influence towards Asia, and acknowledging that the IMF and countries in other regions could learn from Asia – a remarkable turn-around in outlook in just over 10 years time:

"We also want to *listen to what Asia has to say*—about issues and challenges in this region, but also about the policy priorities for countries in other regions. Countries all over the world want to understand how Asia has managed its growth and globalization so successfully. Drawing the lessons of Asia's many successes is an important objective ..."[21]

In terms of rhetorical style, and public relations savvy, Strauss-Kahn's efforts to present the IMF as an institution much more open to Asia influence and viewpoints are quite effective. The question which remains to be seen, however, is to what extent this will translate into meaningful policy and/or governance changes.

Evolving Policies

From a policy perspective, there is already evidence of shifts taking place. As previously described, a number of IMF policy prescriptions mandated during the Asian Financial Crisis were viewed in Asia as unnecessarily harsh and also simply bad economics. Prominent among these policies was the IMF strong stand against the imposition of capital controls in emerging markets, which Malaysia famously defied.

From the China's perspective, anything which could even potentially circumscribe its ability to maintain the RMB exchange rate at a level it deems appropriate would be anathema. Capital controls and other techniques to manipulate currency levels are an important part of China's policy arsenal.

It is interesting therefore to consider the IMF's policy shift which took place in February 2010, with the release of an IMF paper entitled: "Capital Inflows: the Role of Controls". In reversing its earlier stance, the IMF demonstrated that its view had evolved more closely in line with the Chinese view:

"There may be circumstances in which capital controls are a legitimate component of the policy response to surges in capital inflows... If the economy is operating near potential, if the level of reserves is adequate, if the exchange rate is not undervalued, and if the flows are likely to be transitory, then use of capital controls is justified as one element of the policy toolkit to manage inflows." [22]

---

[21] Ibid.

[22] Jonathan D. Ostry, Atish R.Gosh, Karl Habermeier, Marcos Chamen, Mahuash S . Quresh, and Dennis B.S. Reinhardt, "Capital Inflows: The Role of Controls, http://www.imf.org/external/pubs/ft/spn/2010/spn1004.pdf

Chinese views on currency issues are well known and forcefully articulated by its officials, and by the top-notch representatives it sends to the IMF and other institutions. It seems unlikely that the IMF's policy reversal on currency controls was entirely unrelated or merely incidental to China's position.

Case Study

IMF Article IV Consultations

The IMF conducts annual consultations with member countries known as Article IV consultations. This includes a staff visit to the country, a thorough review of macro-economic data and consultations with the appropriate high level government officials, central bank officials, policy makers, and other experts. One of the objectives of these consultations and discussions is to determine if there are "risks" which "argue for adjustments in economic or financial policy".[23]

Article IV consultations provide perhaps the most explicit opportunity for the IMF to review its member's macroeconomic policies, and to make an assessment as to the suitability of those policies.

Article IV Consultations with China were concluded last July. The staff level consultations concluded that the renminbi was "substantially" undervalued. According to Nigel Chalk, the IMF's mission chief, China's currency "remains substantially below the level that's consistent with medium terms fundamentals".[24]

An emphatic assessment by the IMF that the renminbi was substantially undervalued would provide the US with a credible multilateral endorsement of the arguments it has made in bilateral consultations with China.

Under the IMF Articles of Agreement, after staff level consultations are completed, the staff prepares a report and the findings are passed to the IMF Executive Board, which is chaired by

---

[23] Articles of Agreement of the International Monetary Fund, http://www.imf.org/external/pubs/ft/aa/index.htm

[24] Nigel Chalk, "IMF Executive Board Concludes 2010 Article IV Consultation with China", Public Information Notice (PIN) No. 10/100, July 26, 2010;

the IMF Managing Director. In this instance, however, the Executive Board came to a somewhat different conclusion, pointing out that a number of the directors in fact disagreed with the staff assessment, and providing a much more mixed viewpoint on the currency issue. The precise nature of the deliberations at the Executive Board, and the manner in which these decision were reached, is not made public. Disagreement at the Executive Board level has the effect of weakening pressure on China to further strengthen the renmimbi.

Greater Institutional Clout: staffing and voting

Recent high-level staff appointment of Chinese officials at both the World Bank and the IMF are good indications of China's growing economic clout as well as its heightened influence within these institutions.

In 2008, Justin Lin Yifu, a Beijing professor, was appointed to the influential post of Chief Economist of the World Bank.[25] This prominent position has previously been occupied by the likes of Nobel Prize winner Joseph Stiglitz, and former US Treasury Secretary Larry Summers.

Dr. Lin's economic philosophy, however, differs in some important respects from those of his recent predecessors, particularly on the role of government in the economic sphere. Lin has written that "government is the most important institution in determining whether development is successful."[26] He seems also to have clear views on the potential role that China can play in sharing its economic policies and successes. In an interview with *China Business News*, Lin commented that "China is in a unique position to re-write the macro-economic policies of the past". He went on to say that "Because of China's success in transforming the economy and sustaining its growth for a long time, everybody wants to know the formula."[27]

Even just a decade ago, it probably would have been unfathomable that someone with a Masters Degree in Marxist Political Economy from Beijing University (as Lin has) could ascend to such a position

---

[25] Martin Jacques, "Chinese in top job at World Bank", China Daily, June 3, 2008, http://www.chinadaily.com.cn/business/2008-06/03/content_6731511.htm

[26] Bezlova, Antoaneta. "Lin Yifu's World Bank Job May Add To China's Clout." Inter Press Service. January 31, 2008, http://ipsnews.net/print.asp?idnews=41010

[27] Antoaneta Bezlova, "Lin Yifu's World Bank Job May Add to China's Clout", http://ipsnews.net/print.asp?idnews=41010

of power within the World Bank, a traditional bastion of Western economic orthodoxy. The historical philosophical "lock" that the Washington Consensus has held on multilateral development institutions is beginning to loosen.[28]

Senior appointment at IMF

The World Bank's sister organization, the IMF, has seen an even more recent high-level appointment go to a Chinese official. Earlier this year, Zhu Min, deputy governor of the People's Bank of China, was appointed as special advisor to the Managing Director. This is the most senior position held by China within the IMF.[29]

China's central bank issued a statement saying that "the appointment shows emerging nations taking a bigger role in a changing global economic order", while Strauss-Khan, the IMF managing director concurred, saying that Zhu will help the IMF meet "challenges facing our global membership in the period ahead, and in strengthening the fund's understanding of Asia, and emerging markets more generally."[30]

From China's perspective, a more substantial staffing presence with the IMF is clearly both a reflection of the economic power shift from West to East, and a means to "improve" the functioning of the IMF. China's central bank went on to say that appointing emerging market professionals "meets the need for international financial institutions to adapt to changes in the global economic order and is an important step in improving their governance structures."[31]

This appointment can be seen as part of a strategy to put more of a Chinese "stamp" on the institution. According to the Brookings Institution: "China has long sought representation at high-level positions at the IMF as a way of influencing IMF policies and increasing its direct influence in the process of setting the global economic policy agenda".[32]

For two organizations historically dominated by Americans and Europeans, these appointments signal the start of a new era at both the IMF and the World Bank.

---

[28] "Chinese professor named World Bank chief economist", Washington (AFP), February 4, 2008, http: //afp.google.com/article/ALeqM5h-J1IKQZ_r-4SukILjHli-BvFxZw

[29] "IMF Names Zhu Min as Adviser, Showing China's Clout (Update1)", Bloomberg Businessweek, July 21, 2010.

[30] Ibid.

[31] Ibid.

[32] Ibid.

What does it mean?

The "Big Question" of course is what impact senior level appointments such as these will have on the policies of either institution. Although it will take some time before a definitive answer emerges, a few points are worth making.

By way of background, bear in mind that, at least in theory, when an individual takes a position at an international institution that person has become in effect an "international civil servant," working first and foremost for the interests of that particular organization. Except for the designated country representatives, who are there explicitly to pursue national interests, staff should not be advancing a national agenda on behalf of their native country. So Robert Zoellick, for instance, in his capacity as President of the World Bank, should not be, in any way, shape, or form, an advocate for U.S. government positions, despite his long and distinguished career as a senior U.S. diplomat. As with most policy-related issues, there could probably be a lively debate on the extent to which this is actually true, but it is important to recognize that at least in theory, this is the way things are supposed to work, irrespective of whether the appointee is Canadian, Indonesian, Brazilian, or any other nationality.

This dimension take on an added layer of complexity however when looking at Chinese appointees. For any Chinese official who could compete successfully for a senior level appointment at an international organization, the likelihood is that this individual would also be a member of the Communist Party of China. So there could be greater difficulty for these individuals to pursue or advocate policies not in-sync with the Communist Party – which, in a one party system such as China, is wholly synonymous with the Chinese Government.

In fairness it must be acknowledged that any international civil servant – French, South African, American, or Indian -- could be susceptible to the pull of divided loyalties. But it must likewise be acknowledged that there are particular aspects of the Chinese political system and political culture which make it considerably more difficult for a Chinese official -- as opposed to say, a Swedish official -- to completely take off a "national hat" and replace it with an "institutional hat." It would be naive to suggest otherwise, and this fundamental reality must be borne in mind as China becomes increasingly able to lay claim to the top spots at international institutions.

CASE STUDY

Voting Rights: A Bigger Say for China

The governance mechanisms of the International Monetary Fund (IMF) and the World Bank are somewhat complex. Decisions are made through a weighted voting system. All members of the IMF may become members of the WB. Countries seeking entrance into the Fund provide economic data, which is then compared with the figures for other countries with similar-sized economies. The new member is given a quota that corresponds to its subscription to the Fund. This quota indicates the country's voting power in the IMF. Every new member of the WB is given a base of 250 votes plus an additional vote for every share it has of the Bank's capital stock. [33]

The member's quota in the Fund determines the number of shares that are allotted to the new Bank member. The five biggest Bank shareholders – today, they are the United States, Japan, Germany, France and the United Kingdom – appoint five executive directors. China, the Russian Federation and Saudi Arabia each choose an executive director, while other members elect the remaining executive directors. Within the World Bank Group, voting power allocation varies according to agency.

IMF quota reform has been in the works since September 2009, when leaders at the G20 summit in Pittsburgh agreed that there should be a shift of at least 5% from "over-represented countries" to "under-represented countries," notably the "dynamic emerging markets and developing countries." Prior to this decision, developing economies held 43% of the voting rights in the IMF and 44% of the voting rights in the WB. Once the quota reforms go through, developing and so-called transiting countries would have a 47% voting share.

---

[33] Xin, Zhou and Chris Buckley. "China Wants Support on IMF Voting at G20." Reuters, September 15, 2009 http://www.reuters.com/assets/print?aid=USTRE58E29D20090915

At the IMF and WB annual spring meeting in Washington, DC, in April 2010, members decided to increase voting rights of key developing and transiting nations, including India, Mexico, Brazil and China. China's voting share would increase from 2.77% to 4.42%, which would rank it third in terms of voting power. The planned quota adjustments are expected to be finalized at the G20 Summit in Seoul in November and implemented by January 2011. At the BRIC Summit in April, the four emerging economies in the group called for the reforms to be implemented sooner.

Growing assertiveness

China's assertiveness in international organizations has grown in tandem with its increased economic might. In previous years, the official statements and representations of Chinese officials would tend to be narrowly focused on programs and projects directly affecting China. China generally would not wade too deeply into organizational issues, and criticisms were generally minimal.

China's growing assertiveness seemed to hit somewhat of a "tipping point" with the Global financial crisis, and today, whatever lingering hesitancy Chinese officials may have felt in confronting the developed world in general and multilateral development institutions in particular is now a thing of the past.

The comments below, by Dr. Zhou Xiaochuan, Governor of the People's Bank of China, at the International Monetary and Financial Committee in April of 2010, provides a good example of this shift.

When one consider the "diplomatic niceties" and bureaucratic double-speak that usually typify the official statements of senior officials to the IMF, the passage below is striking for its directness and almost combative tone. In essence, Zhou is saying: The West caused the economic crisis, and the focus of the IMF is wrong and needs to be fixed. To quote Zhou (emphasis added):

"At present, **the primary risks to the global economy come from developed countries.** Sovereign debt risk has become a major and real threat to global financial stability and economic recovery, and its potential systemic effects deserve a high degree of attention and concern.

The Fund's purpose is to promote trade, employment, and growth in real income. **The current global financial crisis, which is primarily the result of the inappropriate financial sector in developed countries,** has impacted global trade, employment, and income in an unprecedented manner, and the unsustainability (sic) of developed countries' fiscal policies has become the primary risk that threatens global financial stability. **In recent years, the focus of Fund surveillance has been inappropriate. The hastily introduced 2007 Decision contains many flaws,** and cannot meet the demands on Fund surveillance posed by global economic and financial development. **The Fund should face this reality, resolve the problems in its surveillance as quickly as possible..."** [34]

---

[34] Statement by Dr. ZHOU Xiaochuan Governor of the People's Bank of China at the Twenty-First Meeting of the International Monetary and Financial Committee Washington D.C., April 24, 2010 http://www.cbrc.gov.cn/english/home/jsp/docView.jsp?docID=201010127105895E82201

China as a Competing Source of Developmental Aid: Fast, Effective and No Conditions

The sheer competence and speed with which China is able to negotiate and execute its development programs is an important element of its appeal, and presents a stark contrast with the manner in which similar programs are executed by multilateral institutions.

Government officials from throughout the developing world can typically recite a litany of examples in which aid projects being implemented through Western channels become bogged down in bureaucracy, or are delayed, and in some cases never completed, while similar projects executed by the Chinese are frequently completed ahead of schedule and with a high degree of efficiency.

And of critical importance to at least some countries, there are no questions or demands with regard to "internal issues" or governance structures. On a variety of levels, the "Chinese approach" simply makes more sense to many developing countries.

Abdoulaye Wade, the President of Senegal, writing in the Financial Times of London in 2008, expressed the view and experiences of many of his developing world colleagues with remarkable clarity when he said:

"China's approach to our needs is simply better adapted than the slow and sometimes patronising post-colonial approach of European investors, donor organisations and non-governmental organisations. In fact, the Chinese model for stimulating rapid economic development has much to teach Africa."[35]

Later in the same article, Wade took a swipe not only at the efficiency and effectiveness of multilateral lending institutions, but the "Big Club" of developed countries, the G-8, as well:

"I have found that a contract that would take five years to discuss, negotiate and sign with the World Bank takes three months when we have dealt with Chinese authorities. I am a firm believer in good governance and the rule of law. But when bureaucracy and senseless red tape impede our ability to act – and when poverty persists while international functionaries drag their feet – African leaders have an obligation to opt for swifter solutions. I achieved more in my one hour meeting with President Hu Jintao in an executive suite at my hotel in Berlin during the recent G8 meeting in Heiligendamm than I did during the entire, orchestrated meeting of world leaders at the summit – where African leaders were told little more than that G8 nations would respect existing commitments."[36]

---

[35] Abdoulaye Wade, Senegal's President, "Time for the west to practice what it preaches", Financial Times, January 23, 2008, http://www.ft.com/cms/s/5d347f88-c897-11dc-94a6-0000779fd2ac,dwp_uuid=8735dcb2

[36] Ibid.

As China's financial wherewithal and foreign currency reserves continue to increase, its ability to present itself as a viable alternative to multilateral institutions also increases, and China's lack of conditionality means that it is oftentimes a more attractive source of financial aid and assistance. The net result is that in future years there will likely be a greater number of scenarios, regions, and countries in which China will be able to displace the World Bank and the IMF. A couple of brief examples are illustrative, and suggest that the process is already underway:

In September of 2008, the World Bank canceled an oil pipeline deal with Chad because of a dispute over the extent to which profits would be used for poverty reduction. The lion's share of government spending in Chad had been directed toward the security forces, and without adequate guarantees that the proceeds from the oil pipeline would not be funneled in the same direction, the World Bank backed off.

If officials in Chad experienced any degree of anxiety over this cancelation, it certainly did not last long. A few short weeks later, a senior Chinese official formally announced an official program of closer cooperation with Chad in trade politics, culture, and education to "promote solidarity and common prosperity."[37]

In the Asia region, Cambodia also provides an interesting case in point. While aid from multilateral sources has in some cases been reduced to Cambodia as a result of concerns over human rights practices and governance, these losses have been largely off-set by increasing aid from China. In 2006, Premier Wen Jiabao announced over $600 million of loans and grants to Cambodia as part of its initiative to strengthen relations with Southeast Asia.[38]

More recently, in April of 2010, the United States suspended military aid to Cambodia as a protest in response to the deportation of 20 Uyghur refugees to China. [39] The deportees had been placed under the protection of the UN High Commissioner for Refugees, and were seeking refugee status in Cambodia. Less than a month after Cambodia returned the refugees to China, China pledged over $14 million in military assistance to Cambodia, explicitly as a replacement for the canceled aid from the United States.[40]

---

[37] Halper, page 75

[38] "China Pledges More Military Aid to Cambodia." Asian Political News, May 3, 2010
http://findarticles.com/p/articles/mi_m0WDQ/is_2010_May_3/ai_n53397127/?tag=content;col1.6.

[39] "U.S Cuts Military Aid to Cambodia for Deporting Uyghurs to China." Asian Political News, April 5, 2010
http://findarticles.com/p/articles/mi_m0WDQ/is_2010_April_5/ai_n53035608/?tag=content;col1

[40] "China Pledges More Military Aid to Cambodia." Asian Political News, May 3, 2010
http://findarticles.com/p/articles/mi_m0WDQ/is_2010_May_3/ai_n53397127/?tag=content;col1.6.

It is important to note that China is emerging as an alternative to the IMF not only through its bilateral programs, but also by its nascent effort to establish a multi-lateral Asia-based alternative. In 2009, ASEAN plus 3 agreed to the establishment of a US\$ 120 billion regional reserve fund. China and Japan will be the two largest contributors, with each country providing 32% of the total.[41]

This initiative is still in its formative stages, with discussions and negotiations underway on the functioning of the fund, so it is too soon to draw any conclusions. But this initiative holds at least the potential to establish something along the lines of an "Asian IMF" – one which does not include the United States, and given the predominant role that China is likely to play, would be unlikely to precisely mirror the Washington Consensus-based policy prescriptions and conditionality that China objects to in other multilateral institutions.

As China successfully positions itself as an alternative to Western/IMF/WB development assistance, the primacy and relevance of these institutions is both subtly and not-so-subtly eroded. The World Bank and the IMF are no longer the only, or even necessarily the most important, source of aid and assistance. The availability of funding from China provides countries in the developing world with the ability to bypass the IMF. In order to maintain their relevance, these institutions in effect need to "compete" for "clients," i.e. countries willing to accept IMF/WB assistance and conditionality.

As this "competition" for clients and relevance plays out across the developing world, it will be instructive to track the strategies these organizations adopt to respond to the increased "competition." Pressure for increased efficiency and competence in delivering aid programs would obviously be supported by all, and would therefore be an unambiguously positive by-product of China's aid programs and practices.

But to what extent will there be pressure to water down the conditionality provisions, which are viewed as overly onerous from the perspective of many in the developing world? One thing is certain: China, an increasing influential member of these institutions, is unlikely to object to any weakening of conditionality.

[41] Foroohar, Rana, and Melinda Liu. "It's China's World We're Just Living In It." Newsweek, Mach 12, 2010 http://www.newsweek.com/id/234928/output/print

<u>*CASE STUDY*</u>

A Bold Chinese Proposal:

Zhou Calls for Dollar to be replaced as reserve currency by IMF SDRs

In March 2009, the highly respected Governor of the People's Bank of China, Zhou Xiaochuan, issued a proposal to replace the dollar as the global reserve currency by expanding the use of the "special drawing rights," or SDRs – something of a virtual currency created by the International Monetary Fund, whose value is determined by a basket of major currencies. SDRs had originally been conceived to be a shared currency for international reserves but are mainly used as a way to manage the accounting for the transactions of the IMF with its members.

"When a national currency is used in pricing primary commodities, trade settlements and is adopted as a reserve currency globally, efforts of the monetary authority issuing such a currency to address its economic imbalances by adjusting exchange rate would be made in vain, as its currency serves as a benchmark for many other currencies," Zhou explained in an essay entitled "Reform the International Monetary System" that was released on the PBOC website. "While benefiting from a widely accepted reserve currency, globalization also suffers from the flaws of such a system. The frequency and increasing intensity of financial crises following the collapse of the Bretton Woods system suggests the costs of such a system to the world may have exceeded its benefits. The price is becoming increasingly higher, not only for the users, but also for the issuers of the reserve currencies. Although crisis may not necessarily be an intended result of the issuing authorities, it is an inevitable outcome of the institutional flaws."[42]

The expansion of the SDRs would necessarily bolster the role of the IMF in monitoring and managing the global financial system. This would be in line with China's general support for a more multilateral approach to global governance that was not dominated by the United States or any one country.

The proposal to replace the dollar as the global reserve currency, made as it was by PBOC Governor Zhou, a former state-owned commercial bank chief who is well regarded outside China, was taken seriously around the world as a sign that Beijing was pushing back on

---

[42] Zhou Xiaochuan, "Reform the International Monetary System", People Bank of China, March 2009.

criticism of its currency regime and the management of its financial system and economy, particularly by the United States.

Indeed, in 2008, just days after the Lehman Brothers collapse, another respected state official and former banker criticized the United States for mismanagement and lax surveillance. He noted that, while China's critics would always sound dire warnings of overheating in the economy and the possible bursting of real-estate bubbles, the monetary authorities in Beijing were vigilant to such threats and always took appropriate action when necessary. And even when they did act, they would be criticized for letting the situation get to the point where they had to take certain measures to cool down the economy. The point is, said the former banker, China took action whenever it had to. Meanwhile, he remarked, the global crisis revealed the folly of the U.S. central bank, the Federal Reserve, allowing credit to flow so easily and tolerating the expansion of the sub-prime mortgage market, the collapse of which was one of the factors that led to the financial meltdown in the United States.

Still, the likelihood of the dollar being replaced as the global reserve currency anytime soon is considered low. The SDR proposal is under discussion in financial sector circles, but nothing concrete has emerged besides the suggestion that SDRs might be used to provide emergency liquidity in times of crisis. With the European and Japanese economies and currencies weak, the dollar has if anything bolstered its position as the preferred safe haven in times of crisis, despite the deep economic troubles in the United States. But China's voice has been heard and Zhou's proposal certainly raised the debate over the future of the dollar to a higher level.

Against this backdrop, it is important to note the rumors that, in a year or two, the IMF could have its first Chinese deputy managing director. The appointment in October 2009 of Bank of China vice president and veteran economist Zhu Min to be deputy governor of the PBOC stirred speculation that he was in line for the IMF job after a period learning the ropes at the Chinese central bank. In February 2010, the speculation intensified when IMF Managing Director Dominique Strauss-Kahn named Zhu to be one of his special advisers.

The talk now is that Zhu, who has become well known among on the Davos circuit for his plain speaking English, could even be on track to replace Strauss-Kahn should the Frenchman decide to return home to run for president of his country in 2012.[43] The stranglehold that Europe has had on the IMF managing director's seat would have to be broken for that to happen. But with the mood in the international community -- especially among the G20, the de facto managers of the global economy -- leaning towards greater voice and representation

---

[43] Interview with longtime Davos participant.

for emerging economies, it cannot be completely ruled out. Certainly, the Chinese leadership is grooming Zhu Min for a bigger international role.

Conclusion

China's approach to international financial institutions is clear and sensible, and can be summarized in the following 3 points:

1) Push for, and accept, any opportunities to increase internal institutional influence through increased representation, staffing, and assertiveness.

2) At the same time, however, recognize that it is questionable how significantly the practices and policies of these organizations can be shifted, due both to institutional impediments and to their firm ideological grounding in the principles expressed by the Washington consensus.

3) Therefore, while working to increase influence **within** these organizations, work simultaneously to shift influence **away** from them by the establishment of alternate vehicles, either on a bilateral or regional basis.

This strategy places pressure both on the primacy of the IMF/WB role in the global system, as well as the sustainability of their traditional policies and governance structures within these organizations.

The Asia Pacific Economic Cooperation (APEC) Forum

Background

Founded in 1989 to promote trade, investment, and a sense of regional identity and cooperation amongst the leading economies of the Asia-Pacific region, the Asia Pacific Economic Cooperation Forum (APEC) has grown into arguably one of the most important governmental organizations in the region.

The over-arching mission of the organization is derived from the "Bogor Goals" (established in Bogor, Indonesia in 1994), which call for free and open trade and investment by 2010 for developed members, and by 2020 for developing members. Most of APEC's work is conducted through its so-called 3 pillars: 1) trade and investment liberalization; 2) business facilitation; and 3) economic and technical cooperation.[44]

APEC is a voluntary organization, reaching decisions by consensus, and all of the commitments are non-binding in nature. In that sense, APEC is fundamentally different from the World Trade Organization. Over the years, the APEC agenda has expanded substantially, and now includes issues such as climate change, public health, and counter-terrorism. [45]

The Two Dimensions of APEC

In attempting to fully comprehend China's role in APEC, it is useful to think about APEC on two levels. There is the high profile and widely covered annual leaders meeting, which brings together the political leaders with senior executives from the business world, and which focuses mostly on broad issues.

The other level on which APEC operates is the working level, which is more mundane but arguably more impactful. Although the leaders only gather once a year, an army of officials and bureaucrats labor on an ongoing basis throughout the course of the year on a wide range of specific issues. Work groups and tasks forces have been established and are pursuing active agendas in areas such as Agricultural Technical Cooperation, Energy, Fisheries, Health, Industrial Science and Technology, Telecommunications, Transportation, and Anti-Corruption and Transparency [46]

Although rarely making it into the headlines, the work which emerges from these sector-specific or issue-specific groups constructively advance the agenda in a steady, albeit incremental way.

The distinction between the political level and the technical working level will be important to bear in mind when we look at China's role and involvement in APEC, as China's approach can vary widely between these two different tracks.

---

[44] "APEC at a Glance". APEC, 2010

[45] Ibid.

[46] Ibid.

China's involvement in APEC: What does China "want"?

Perhaps the best way to explore the nature of China's involvement in APEC is to start by posing two deceptively simple questions: what does China want from APEC, and perhaps more importantly, what does China want to avoid in APEC?

In terms of what China wants, APEC's third pillar – economic and technical cooperation – seems to be most relevant. As can be seen in a number of the organizations in which it participates, China has been remarkably effective in using its intuitional memberships as a means to access knowledge and technical know-how that it considers to be important to its ongoing economic development.

As reported by Xinhua, Minister Shi Guangsheng, then minister of foreign trade and economic cooperation, clearly outlined China's approach to APEC:

"Participation in the APEC process will also offer opportunities for China to learn advanced science and technology and managerial expertise from other APEC members, Shi said, adding that his country has already learnt a lot in areas like government procurement, international electronic business administration, and customs procedures.   By increasing economic and technological cooperation with other APEC economies, Shi said, China will be able to keep abreast with the latest developments in the world's scientific and technical fields, raising higher its own technical levels." [47]

 The APEC Agricultural Technical Cooperation Working Group (ATCWG) -- whose objective is to "enhance agriculture's contribution to the region's economic growth and social well-being by promoting agricultural technical cooperation between APEC members" -- provides an excellent example of precisely what Minister Shi describes. [48]

China has taken a leadership role within this group, serving as Chair for this extremely active committee which concerns itself with a number of issues of great developmental importance to China. The ATCWG draws on the expertise of both government officials and academic experts from APEC member economies.

Among the objectives and areas of activity for the ATCWG is improving capacity within agricultural industries to share information and experiences in related areas such as biotechnology, and animal and biogenetic resource management.   More specifically, the group has tackled issues such as: strengthening food safety standards; responding to food security challenges; promoting the

---

[47] "Chinese participation in APEC Significant: Minister", People's Daily Online, http://english.peopledaily.com.cn/english/200110/16/print20011016_82414.html

[48] "China's Participation in APEC Significant: Minister." People's Daily. October 16, 2001

development of next-generation sustainable biofuels; enhancing agriculture's ability to adjust and mitigate the impact of climate change; and strengthening technological cooperation in the strategic planning of ATCWG projects.[49]

The reasons for China's active engagement and leadership within this group are self-evident. From the domestic Chinese perspective, the issue of food safety could hardly be more important. A spate of recent scandals involving tainted food products engendered deep civil distress across China, and registered at the highest levels of the Chinese government. The existing food safety system in China is disjointed, complex, and notoriously unresponsive.

Among the recent food safety incidents have been the improper use of pesticides or other chemicals, dangerous additives used as food preservers, and unhygienic materials and practices. The most serious breach was the milk scandal in 2008, which included milk and infant formula contaminated by melamine. It affected an estimated 300,000 victims, with six infants dying from kidney related damage, and over 800 babies hospitalized.[50]

Chinese Vice Premier Li Keqiang, speaking at a State Council meeting earlier this year said: "Food is essential, and safety should be a top priority. Food safety is closely related to people's lives and health and economic development and social harmony... We must create a food safety system of self-disciplined food companies with integrity, effective government supervision and broad public support, to improve overall food safety." He went on to urge improvements in food safety standards, production inspections and emergency responses.[51]

On this, and a wide range of other issue-areas, China is actively and constructively working within the APEC system, bringing benefits both to China and to the organization.

The second question -- "What does China want to avoid in APEC?" -- is a bit more complex. As previously noted, APEC's broad mission is to act as a vehicle for trade and investment liberalization throughout the region, and it pursues this goal -- albeit with mixed success -- through its various activities and initiatives under the direction of the APEC ministers and leaders.

But it is fair to question the extent to which China would actually like to see APEC fully realize this goal. Is it in China's interests to see APEC -- an organization which includes the United States -- become the region's preeminent platform for facilitating economic integration though trade and investment liberalization? A stronger APEC necessarily brings with it a stronger US role in the region. These sentiments and misgivings are likely heightened by the presence of a separate seat at the APEC table for

---

[49] ATCWG webpage: http://www.apec.org/apec/apec_groups/som_committee_on_economic/working_grou ps/agricultural_technical.html

[50] "China Vows New Food Safety Campaign", Xinhua, October 2, 2010.

[51] Ibid.

Chinese Taipei, i.e. Taiwan. How realistic would it be to expect China to embrace and support a stronger APEC?

It is interesting to note that China nonetheless frequently assumes a stance within internal APEC operational deliberations that discourages or delays initiatives or proposals which could – however modestly – enhance APEC's institutional strength. This could be on issues as mundane as expanding permanent staff positions, or appointing staff to work on policy issues which are typically supportive of greater trade and investment liberalization. It is common for there to be a lot of questioning as to the nature and need for such positions, and a general advocacy of a go-slow approach on things which could even just marginally provide APEC with greater institutional strength.

Bear this in mind though: Given APEC's inherent institutional weaknesses – a far-flung, geographically and economically diverse organization which operates on consensus and steers clear of controversy – China would not need to be terribly proactive or obstructionist to ensure that the organization remains mired on the big issue of regional free trade. The very nature of APEC ensures that that will likely be the case, irrespective of what China does, or does not, do.

Rather than see APEC enhance its capacity and play a predominant role, it makes far greater strategic sense for China to strengthen other institutions or groupings in the hope that they can eventually usurp the APEC vision.

To the extent that APEC's efforts to achieve anything even remotely approaching regional free trade remain in a state of stasis, member economies inevitably grow restive, and turn their gaze elsewhere. This same dynamic can be seen at play on the global stage, where the dormancy of the Doha Round, has caused countries to opt instead for bilateral or regional FTAs. To the extent APEC members come to believe that APEC is incapable of acting as the primary driver on the broad issue of regional free trade, the prominence and the relevance of alternatives is heightened.

ASEAN/ASEAN + 3

The most attractive alternative formulation from China's perspective is likely ASEAN/ASEAN + 3, which provides coverage of the most important markets in the region. The obvious advantages are that such an approach removes the US – and its oftentimes confrontational agenda – from the equation; it undermines US economic linkages in the region, and obviates issues surrounding the inclusion of Taiwan.

The China-ASEAN Free Trade Area, signed in Phnom Penh in 2005, is instructive. The agreement brought together the 10 members of ASEAN and China, with the goal of establishing fully implemented free trade by the beginning of 2010. Covering more than 1.8 billion people, this FTA is the world's largest in terms of population; and amounting to a combined $6 trillion in GDP, it is the third largest after the European Economic Area and NAFTA.[52]

In one stroke, this agreement accomplished several things: it provides China with access to the raw materials it needs to fuel its continued growth, it helps secure vital sea lanes, and it establishes an extremely important regional economic institution that excludes both the United States and its major regional allies. By moving the ball significantly further than APEC has done, this agreement undermines an organization in which the United States is a major player, and which provides a separate seat for Taiwan.

The other advantage of an approach like this is that it moves the game onto a platform that is less fraught with issues that China is either less concerned about, or uncomfortable about addressing. Although APEC was originally intended as a forum to discuss only economic issues, the agenda has evolved, particularly in the aftermath of the September 11 terrorist attacks in 2001, to increasingly include security issues, and other non-economic issues. These can be problematic from China's perspective because they can brush against the strongly held Chinese aversion to anything which even hints at "interference" in a country's internal affairs. In fairness though, it should be noted that in the immediate aftermath of the September 11 attacks, China was largely supportive of the need to discuss security issues during the Shanghai Leaders' Meeting, held just a month later, although needless to say, not with the same degree of fervor the United States attached to the issue.

In sum, China's approach to APEC is to:

1) Constructively engage the forum on those levels that can provide benefits to China – principally the acquisition of technical know-how and international best practices. China also effectively engages APEC as a stage on which to project its growing economic and strategic influence, both to a domestic and international audience.

2) China is however much more ambivalent about APEC's vision of establishing itself as the predominant vehicle in the region for trade and investment liberalization; and increasingly, on a wider range of other strategic issues not necessarily economic in nature. While not wanting to be seen as obstructionist, China can nevertheless be expected to effectively exploit APEC's inherent inability to act decisively in order to help ensure that the organization never fully achieves its broader vision.

---

[52] Brown, Kevin. "Biggest Regional Trade Deal Unveiled", Financial Times, January 1, 2010.

CASE STUDY

Soft Power in APEC

As with any regional or international organization, there can be important "soft power" aspects to APEC. In essence, soft power connotes the ability of a nation to lead by virtue of its attractiveness, by virtue of its ability to inspire admiration and a desire on the part of others to be "more like you." Countries which successfully wield soft power are those which are viewed as somehow "impressive" on variety of different levels.

In recent years, China has increasingly used APEC as a forum to skillfully promote and develop its soft power. In October of 2001, in the immediate aftermath of the September 11 terrorist attacks in the United States, China hosted the APEC Leaders Meeting in the booming metropolis of Shanghai. The worldwide media attention on this event, which is fairly intensive in any year, was even greater given the fact that this was the first major gathering of international leaders since the tragic attacks. All eyes were focused on Shanghai.

To any long-term APEC observer who routinely attends the APEC leaders meeting on a year in, year out basis, the Shanghai meeting stands apart as perhaps the high-water mark, on a number of different levels. First and foremost, on symbolic and impressionistic terms, the city of Shanghai itself spoke volumes about China's stunning economic growth. Although just 20 years ago much of Shanghai was nothing more than farmland, by the time APEC arrived in 2001 the modern, even futuristic skyline of the city, the constant hammering of ongoing construction, the buzz of endless activity, and the kinetic energy of the city, all seemed to easily eclipse that of the region's traditional powerhouses, like Hong Kong, Tokyo, or Singapore.

Because of the growing economic importance of China to so many companies' balance sheets, the APEC CEO Summit attracted an unusually large number of very senior executives from not just the region, but from the world, and the governments of each member economy – the United States in particular – were represented at even higher levels than usual. The critical mass of the event was such that, some senior executives actually changed plans at the last moment to join the meeting in progress, based on the reports they received as the meeting was unfolding There was, in a very palpable sense, a "buzz" to the meeting. In some respects, the delegate list at an APEC meeting serves as a referendum on the importance and influence of the host country. Smaller and less economically or strategically influential countries find it more difficult to attract the highest level officials and executives from the most important *countries. By this measure, the Shanghai meeting was probably to this day the most successful ever.*

The social and recreational amenities, which for better or worse are oftentimes what stick most in participants minds, were nothing short of spectacular -- in particular the closing fireworks display, which is still talked about by participants over 10 years later.

This impressive display – by virtue of the time and circumstances n which it took place, by virtue of the brilliance with which it was organized, and by virtue of the statement made by the city itself – was a classic, perhaps defining example of the concept of soft power. Regardless of whatever notions any participant might have brought to Shanghai, it would have been impossible to leave the city without the strong sense that China had "arrived."

In some respects, China's successful hosting of the APEC leaders meeting in Shanghai in 2001 was a precursor to China's hosting of the Beijing Olympics in 2008, and the current Shanghai World Expo, two events which have been even more impactful in signaling China's arrival to the rest of the world.

Such soft power displays should not be underestimated as a means to shape perceptions and opinions -- both domestically within China, and perhaps more importantly in other nations around the world.

When assessing how China's role in the United Nations has changed since the PRC took control of the China seat in the UN in 1971, it is important to understand the context in which that critical event took place. When the UN was established in 1945, the Kuomintang-run government of the Republic of China, led by Chiang Kai-shek, was in charge. Four years later, the Communists took over in Beijing and the People's Republic of China was founded. The Nationalists withdrew to Taiwan.

From that time, the PRC launched efforts to gain recognition from the UN but was thwarted by the United States and its Western allies who feared the prospect of another Communist regime after the Soviet Union taking one of the permanent seats on the Security Council. Indeed, if the Communist government in Beijing had held China's seat in the UN, it would have blocked the deployment of the UN force on the Korean Peninsula in 1950. In protest of the PRC's exclusion from the United Nations, the USSR boycotted the UN from January 1950 to August 1950, its absence resulting in Security Council approval of the intervention.[53]

Time was on the side of the PRC, however. As more and more developing nations, particularly newly independent states in Africa joined the UN, Beijing's support strengthened. Eventually, other Western countries including the United States itself would come around to the idea that they should reach out to Beijing. On 25 October 1971, United Nations General Assembly Resolution 2578, which recognized the government of the People's Republic of China as the "only legitimate representatives of China," passed – the 21st time that such a resolution had come to a vote. The UN's decision heralded the shift in United States policy towards the PRC. President Richard Nixon visited China the following year. Sino-American ties were normalized in 1979.

Yet for some time after the PRC took control of the China seat, Beijing remained wary of the United Nations, concerned that Washington was using the UN as a Cold War tool. China took a generally passive role in the organization, turning active only when it perceived it to be in its national interest. This was especially the case when Beijing wished to assert its sovereignty over Taiwan, in the face of the Taipei government's attempts to maintain and expand its diplomatic space in the world. With Taiwan and Tibet in mind, the PRC would seek to defend the principle of non-intervention in the internal affairs of a sovereign state. China did not sign the convention to create the International Criminal Court because of its concerns that the ICC would contravene the traditional concept of sovereignty.

---

[53] United Nations, Dag Hammarskjold Library. http://www.un.org/Depts/dhl. Unless otherwise indicated, all historical UN institutional or factual information is contained in Dag Hammarskjold Library.

Table shows number of times veto was cast, by country[54]

Period	China*	France	Britain	US	USSR/Russia	Total
Total	6	18	32	82	124	261
2008	1	-	-	-	1	2
2007	1	-	-	-	1	2
2006	-	-	-	2	-	2
2005	-	-	-	-	-	-
2004	-	-	-	2	1	3
2003	-	-	-	2	-	2
2002	-	-	-	2	-	2
2001	-	-	-	2	-	2
2000	-	-	-	-	-	0
1999	1	-	-	-	-	1
1998	-	-	-	-	-	0
1997	1	-	-	2	-	3
1996	-	-	-	-	-	0
1986-95	-	3	8	24	2	37
1976-85	-	9	11	34	6	60
1966-75	2	2	10	12	7	33
1956-65	-	2	3	-	26	31
1946-55	(1*)	2	-	-	80	83

---

[54] http://www.globalpolicy.org/security-council/tables-and-charts-on-the-security-council-0-82/use-of-the-veto.html#1. Same source for table below on changing patterns in use of veto.

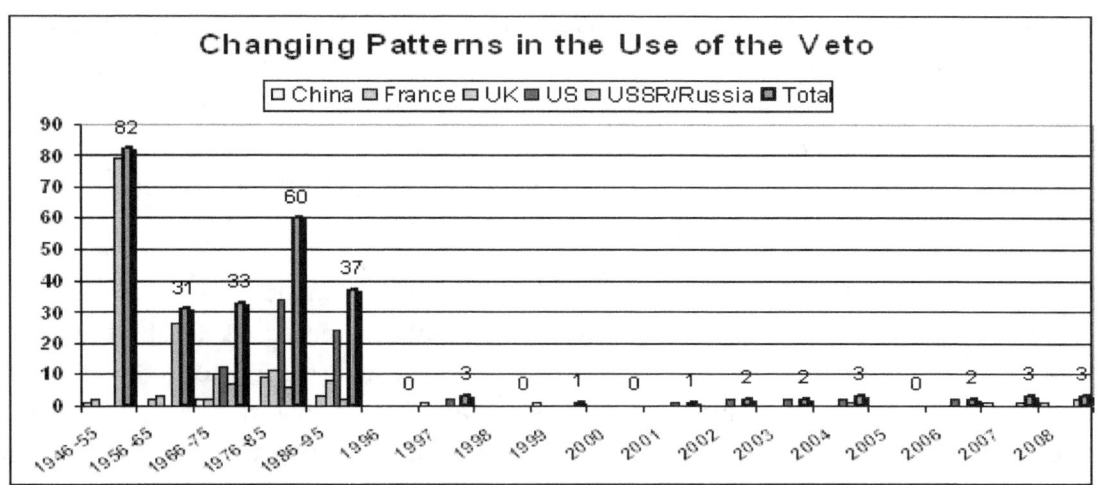

Changing Patterns in the Use of the Veto

While Beijing regards its UN Security Council veto power as bestowing China special status in the international community, the PRC has used it only six times since 1971. China is by a wide margin the member of the permanent five member countries of the UN Security Council (P5) that has employed the veto the least, though since 1995, all of the UNSC permanent members have used it sparingly. In 1972, China blocked the admission to the UN of Bangladesh, which Beijing regarded as a part of Pakistan. A year later, it joined the Soviet Union to veto a resolution calling for a ceasefire in the Yom Kippur War. It did not then use its veto power until 1997 when it rejected a move to send ceasefire observers to Guatemala, which recognized Taipei as the government of China.

In 1999, two weeks after the Former Yugoslav Republic of Macedonia established diplomatic ties with Taipei, which had dangled US$1 billion in investment as a sweetener, China vetoed the extension of the UN peacekeeping mandate in the Balkan country. Security Council members condemned China's action, which Beijing denied was linked to Taiwan's diplomatic coup. Within months, in part due to shifts in the country's domestic politics, Macedonia reverted to recognizing Beijing.[55]

In 2007, together with Russia, China blocked a resolution critical of Myanmar's human rights record. A year later, again with Russia, China vetoed sanctions against Zimbabwe.[56]

Each time it used its veto, China was seeking to make a point regarding its sovereignty over Taiwan, reject international intervention in what it regarded as the internal affairs of a sovereign state, or counter what it perceived to be hegemonic U.S. action.

---

[55] Alexander Casella, "Macedonia: Taiwan's Lost Gambit", *Asia Times Online*, July 11, 2001.

[56] United Nations, Dag Hammarskjold Library. http://www.un.org/Depts/dhl. Unless otherwise indicated, all historical UN institutional or factual information is contained in Dag Hammarskjold Library.

China has also chosen to abstain on critical votes, on which it might have used the veto but could avoid doing so if another P5 member was already going to do so. And it has abstained on crucial votes, thereby avoiding having to go on record as supporting a measure, but not standing in its way, either: Perhaps the best example of this practice was the Gulf War resolution in 1991. China would probably have abstained again if a similar resolution authorizing the use of force against Iraq had been put to a Security Council vote in 2003 before the United States-led invasion of Iraq.

China's relative passivity in the UN Security Council belies its deeper engagement in other aspects of the UN's work. In peacekeeping, for example, China has consistently increased its level of support, participation and commitment since first casting a vote in favor of a resolution to authorize a UN peacekeeping force in Cyprus in 1981.   China has even joined peacekeeping operations in countries such as Haiti that recognize the government on Taiwan. And there are indications that China is now prepared to send combat troops on UN missions, a major commitment for any nation. (See section below on peacekeeping).[57]

China's growing engagement in peacekeeping operations stands in contrast to its much more low-key involvement in conflict resolution, especially given what is often cast by critics as its mercantilist, non-judgmental foreign policy when it comes to conflict zones and certain developing regions such as Africa in which China has a strong commercial interest. The perception among its detractors is that China is willing to block efforts to put pressure on erratic governments or human rights abusers because it is only interested in natural resources, energy and other raw materials.[58] And while there is ample evidence to substantiate this view, there are some subtleties that should not be overlooked. While China has appeared to "coddle" or least shield regimes in Zimbabwe, the Sudan and Myanmar from the rebukes of the West, it has in some cases worked for change behind the scenes. Its rhetoric, however, is usually consistent with the principle that the international community should not interfere in the internal affairs of a sovereign nation, and its actions, either in front of or behind the scenes, still fall considerably short of what the United States and other Western nations would prefer.

All this suggests that China's general attitude towards the UN remains today somewhat ambivalent – perhaps it might best be described oxymoronically as "consistently ambivalent." While Chinese leaders and certainly China's diplomatic establishment regard the United Nations as the pivotal international organization in the world, with unique legitimacy and status – it sends only its very best diplomats to be the country's ambassador in New York – there remains an essentially Asian view that the UN is still dominated by Atlanticists, that the UN and its agencies do not have much impact in Asia, that the US and some other countries in the West are only interested in multilateralism when they can get their way

---

[57] International Crisis Group, "China's Growing Role in UN Peacekeeping", Asia Report No. 166, April 17, 2009.

[58] Ibid

and it suits them, and that China, India and other emerging powers are not well represented inside the organization or on its leadership.

These negative perceptions have moderated somewhat over Ghanaian Kofi Annan's two terms as secretary-general and the ascendance of South Korean foreign minister Ban Ki-moon to replace him. China's support was critical in the appointment of Ban, given that no all the major powers in the UN were swayed by the argument that it was Asia's turn to fill the UNSG seat. Perhaps in recognition of that support, Ban named Sha Zukang, China's former ambassador to the UN in Geneva, to become his under-secretary-general for economic and social affairs.

In the UN, China acts when it cares to do so and sees its interests clearly at stake. China sees the world as still centered on the sovereign state and many its foreign policy stands and decisions will be influenced by its solid positions on Taiwan, Tibet and human rights.

China's ambivalence or ambiguity can be seen in its support for UN reform. While it is for widening permanent membership in the Security Council to include other developing countries (this would presumably exclude Japan), it is loathe to devalue the veto by according to privilege to newcomers. Beijing has vacillated between supporting permanent membership for India but without the veto to rejection after India grouped together with Brazil, Germany and Japan to push for their inclusion.

China has also demonstrated its willingness to contribute more to the UN budget. At the beginning of 2010, China's contributions to the UN regular budget rose from 2.667% of the total to 3.189% - about USD80 million. Its contributions to the peacekeeping budget rose from 3.147% of the total to 3.939%, or about USD300 million.[59] Today, China is the eighth largest contributor to the UN regular budget, behind the seven industrialized countries (Britain, Canada, France, Germany, Italy, Japan and the United States), even though by per capita income, China is barely in the top 100 in the world. China has increased its contributions four times in the past decade.

Telling too is China's support of comprehensive UN reform. It has pushed for the UN to reverse its tendency to give priority to security over development and, in this vein, has been active in supporting and participating in such initiatives as the Millennium Development Goals and agencies such as the United Nations Department of Economic and Social Affairs (UNDESA) and the United Nations Conference on Trade and Development (UNCTAD). China hosted the landmark 4th UN World Conference on Women in 1995 in Beijing, along with a major parallel gathering of NGOS in nearby Huairou, more than 40,000 women attending. Hosting such a large meeting of NGOs was a significant step for China,

---

[59] Andrew F. Cooper and Thomas Fues, "Do the Asian Drivers Pull Their Diplomatic Weight? China, India, and The United Nations", *World Development*, Vol. 36, No. 2, 2008

which has long been wary of engaging with civil society organizations within the context of multilateral state-to-state interaction.[60]

China has long been fond of stressing economic, social and development issues within the UN, pushing for a stronger focus on these "soft" issues rather than on security. China has participated in the activities of the so-called Group of 77 developing nations (now actually about 130) that was launched in 1964 at the inaugural UNCTAD. The G77 is meant to bolster the influence and leverage of developing economies within the UN. While it is now the world's second biggest economy after the United States, China has carefully cast itself as still a developing economy with developing-country problems and developing-nation concerns. It has aligned itself with the developing world, while being mindful not to claim to be its spokesman.

There are signs that China's thinking is gradually evolving, at least on some fronts. China's recent cooperation with UNCTAD on the agency's annual *Economic Development in Africa* report, which focused on "South-South Cooperation: Africa and the New Forms of Development Partnership," suggests that Beijing is willing to be more transparent about its commercial and development relationships in Africa.[61] In fact, UNCTAD, which is headed by former World Trade Organization director-general Supachai Panitchpakdi, who was once a Thai government minister, took advantage of the Shanghai World Expo to hold a seminar in June 2010 to highlight China's growing relationship with Africa, stressing the theme of "cooperation for equitable development".

Beijing is increasingly mindful of its image around the world. It distanced itself from Zimbabwean leader Robert Mugabe when controversy arose over arms sales. The threat of a boycott of the 2008 Beijing Olympics, which was promoted by critics of China who alleged that the PRC was protecting the Sudanese government from pressure by the international community over Darfur, was enough for the Chinese to take the unprecedented steps of dispatching their highly skilled UN ambassador to talk candidly with the regime in Khartoum and appointing a special representative on the Darfur issue. These were the sort of conflict resolution measures that China is not used to taking, even under the umbrella of the United Nations.

What's the Bottom Line?

There has been a subtle progression and evolution discernable in China's approach to the UN, especially as it involves China's relationships on the African continent. China has shown slightly greater transparency, more openness towards intervention, and a bit more sensitivity to its image. But these modest shifts are probably seen as the "price" China must pay to continue to enhance its credibility on

---

[60] "Beijing and its follow-up". United Nations. http://www.un.org/womenwatch/daw/beijing/

[61] "Economic Development in Africa. UNCTAD, 2010
http://www.unctad.org/Templates/WebFlyer.asp?intItemID=5491&lang=1

the international stage, and it remains to be seen whether these steps ultimately prove to be cosmetic or substantive in nature. But in any case – and as has been seen in other examples – the Chinese approach is tactically shrewd.

At this point, the view of China as placing its commercial interests far above humanitarian concerns continues to be most credible, and ongoing Chinese ambivalence towards the UN – which is seen as dominated by the Americans and the Europeans – is still pronounced.

<u>The G-20</u>

The Global Financial Crisis propelled the G-20 from relative obscurity to preeminence seemingly overnight. The driving force behind this rapid ascendancy was a recognition that the existing power structure (as epitomized by the G-8) has declined dramatically in relevance, that rapidly growing developing countries have not been adequately represented to an extent commensurate with their importance in the global economy, and that a broader, more balanced power structure – either within or beyond existing institutions -- is required to effectively deal with current realities and challenges. This is a theme which has been woven throughout the discussion of other, longer- established institutions, and it is a dynamic which implicitly shifts power and influence towards China.

The G-20 provides an especially interesting case study because it contrasts sharply in several respects with most of the other institutions under review. First and foremost, the grouping is still in its infancy. There are no long-standing patterns of behavior or institutional history to review. There is no organizational charter which stipulates precise structures and procedures or which articulate specific objectives or deliverables. Debates are not public, there are no voting rights or member shares, and virtually no institutional staff to discuss and analyze.

The G-20 is being created in real time, right before our eyes.

Although membership in the G-20 is somewhat arbitrary in nature (it does not necessarily reflect the 20 largest economies in the world in any given year) it does undeniably represent an impressive combination of geographic and developmental diversity, as well as an eye-popping cumulative economic power: 90% of global GDP, 80% of world trade, and two-thirds of the world population.[62]

Asia is well represented within the G-20 by China, Japan, South Korea, India, and Indonesia. The other BRIC economies – Brazil and Russia – are also included, as are other rapidly growing developing countries such as Argentina, South Africa, and Turkey. The IMF and the World Bank also participate in the G-20.[63]

It is too early to draw any firm conclusions about how the G-20 will operate and function in its new incarnation as "Executive Committee" for the global economy. It is a disparate and fractious group, and it remains to be seen if there will be enough unity and commonality of purpose to ever actually accomplish anything significant.

It is likewise difficult at this early stage to definitively characterize China's approach and strategy in the G-20. China's G-20 strategy thus far has been one of "wait and see." From the Chinese perspective it

---

[62] "What is the G-20?", G-20 website, www.g20.org/about

[63] ibid

is unclear whether the G-20 will prove to be an effective forum for China to advance its interests, or if it will be a forum in which China comes under pressure on issues such as the value of its currency, and other economic and trade policies. All of this remains to be seen. The Chinese strategy in situations like this is typically to carefully study all the angles and avoid precipitous moves. We are in the early stages of a chess match, and all the key questions are still wide open: which countries will assert leadership, which issues will come to the forefront, and what types of alliances will be formed. The Chinese are, for the most part, keeping their powder dry.

Despite this however, we can discern two noteworthy patterns regarding China and the G-20 which will bear further monitoring as the grouping continues to evolve, and which could have implications for China's conduct in other international institutions:

1. The best defense is sometimes a good offense

Since the G-20's rise to prominence (with the 2009 London Summit) China has demonstrated a firm resolve to avoid being placed on the defensive at Summit meetings, and it has accomplished this by actively going on the offensive. China has skillfully used this strategy to force others back onto their heels, and to change the topic of the conversation.

By issuing last-minute policy pronouncements or high profile public comments just before Summit meetings, China has been able to shift the anticipated terms of the debate. For instance, in the run-up to the most recent G-20 meeting in Toronto, the meeting was widely anticipated to be a showdown on the level of China's currency, the RMB. Political pressure within the US had been intensifying as Congressional leaders revived talk of a punitive tariff on Chinese products to offset what is viewed as an unfair advantage resulting from an undervalued RMB. The U.S. Treasury Department is required to report to Congress every six months on currencies, and was supposed to issue a report to Congress in mid-April, ruling on whether or not China's currency is undervalued.[64] This report was delayed in part to allow the issue to be dealt with in the context of the G-20.

A handful of days before the G-20 meeting was to convene, China announced that it would be introducing greater flexibility into its exchange rate valuation. In economic terms, the impact of this announcement was dubious. The bands within which the currency would float were not widened, so the RMB would not dramatically appreciate.[65] And in fact, it could and actually did depreciate slightly in the first days of the float. The move by China's Central Bank also ruled out the possibility of a steep one-off appreciation of the RMB, something which many in the US had called for. [66]

---

[64] Davis, Bob. "US Presses China on Currency", Wall Street Journal, July 9, 2010.

[65] Geoff Dyer, "Beijing 'steals US thunder' ahead of G20", Financial Times, June 20, 2010.

[66] Ibid.

But in political terms, the effect of the announcement was much more impactful. In one stroke, the contentious issue of RMB valuation was essentially taken off the table during the G-20 discussions, in effect "stealing the thunder" from the United States and other countries that had hoped to use the meeting to apply pressure to China.[67] By moving preemptively on its own, China was able to let just enough air out of the balloon on the currency issue and shift the discussion to issues it was more comfortable with – specifically what the developed world, and the United States in particular, needed to do in order to set their own houses in order.

A similar pattern was seen in the 2009 London Summit. In that instance, China's large current account surplus was expected to be a major agenda item. In the run-up to that meeting, China's Central Bank Governor Zhou Xiaochuan made a trenchant and high-profile public call for the replacement of the U.S. dollar as the world's reserve currency.[68] This statement had the effect of knocking the United States back on its heels, forcing it to defend the stability of the U.S. dollar as the world's reserve currency, and the U.S. government's commitment to maintain its value. Once again, the discussion at the G-20 Summit was tilted away from China and back in the direction of the U.S. economy.

2. Deference to China

The G-20 has, in essence, placed a large "bet" on China. One of the outcomes of the most recent summit meeting in Toronto was the commitment of developed countries (with enough ambiguity left for the United States) to turn their focus from stimulus measures to tackling the massive budget deficits that have been rung up during the response to the crisis. If the developed world (or at least significant segments of the developed world) are moving towards consolidation and away from consumption, the clear presumption upon which all of this is predicated is that China will become an even more important driver of global growth and consumption.[69] It would be an overstatement to say that the G-20 is counting on China to pull the world through this stage of the GFC, but clearly China will be central to the success of the G-20's strategy.

Chinese officials, for their part, have been straightforward in advising their G-20 colleagues not to rely too heavily on China, pointing out that it is still a developing country and cannot be expected to "bail out" its rich G-20 partners. Chinese economic policy makers now seem more focused on cooling off any possible over-heating in the Chinese economy and heading off the formation of asset bubbles that might be forming in the aftermath of China's own stimulus efforts. From China's perspective, maintaining

---

[67] Geoff Dyer, "Beijing 'steals US thunder' ahead of G20", Financial Times, June 20, 2010.

[68] Xiaochuan, Zhou. "Reform the International Monetary System." The People's Bank of China, March 23, 2009, http://www.pbc.gov.cn/english/detail.asp?col=6500&ID=178

[69] Geoff Dyer, "G20 Looks to Beijing to Drive Global Growth", Financial Times, July 11, 2010

growth rates above 8% during the GFC is, in and of itself, a significant contribution to global economic stability.

But irrespective of how much Chinese officials can or will stoke growth and consumption, it is clear that the G-20 "needs" China to give the developed world the required breathing room to repair public and private balance sheets.[70] This dynamic has helped fuel a certain deference to China's priorities and objectives within the G-20, and China has been able to walk away from recent summit meetings feeling that their viewpoint had prevailed on the most important issues.

One of China's key priorities has been to use the G-20 as a forum to push for greater developed world representation at the international financial institutions, and the G-20 did in fact agree to accelerate the IMF reform programs (which would shift greater power to the developing world) by two years – from 2013 to 2011.[71]

A related issue has been China's desire to pry lose the vice-grip that Western countries have on the leadership positions at the World Bank and the IMF. And the G-20 did agree in Toronto to commit to an open, transparent, and merit based selection process for the heads and senior leadership at international financial institutions.[72] It will be very interesting to see how this commitment plays out. While it would be difficult to envision a Chinese Managing Director at the IMF in the near future, it also was difficult just 5 years ago to imagine a Chinese chief economist at the World Bank – and that has come to pass.

There has also been deference to China on "defensive" issues – things that China would like to see dropped from official G-20 agenda or closing communiqués. An early draft of the Toronto Summit communiqué included a section welcoming China's move towards greater exchange rate flexibility. This passage was summarily dropped at China's insistence.[73] Although the proposed reference was entirely positive, China did not want to establish a precedent by which it would become acceptable for the G-20 to offer any commentary – good, bad or otherwise – on China's exchange rate policy. China firmly holds the view that its exchange rate policies are entirely an internal issue and should not be subject to discussion in such an international forum.

While it is still too early to draw any firm conclusions, it's safe to say that, thus far, China has been highly effective in pursuing and achieving its objectives in the G-20.

---

[70] Geoff Dyer, "G20 Looks to Beijing to Drive Global Growth", Financial Times, July 11, 2010

[71] The G-20 Toronto Summit Declaration, June 26-27, 2010

[72] Ibid.

[73] "G20 Drops China Sensitive Plaudits on Yuan Reform." Reuters, June 2010.

CASE STUDY

A Skilled and Effective Negotiator:

China in Copenhagen

The UN Copenhagen Climate Change Conference in December of 2009 was intended to produce a framework agreement for climate change mitigation beyond 2012, as a successor to the Kyoto Protocol. Entering the negotiations, the US and Chinese viewpoints and negotiating objectives were largely divergent. The US favored binding commitments and numerical targets, while China, being at a much earlier stage in its economic development, was primarily concerned about maintaining its flexibility, and limiting any binding commitments which could possibly impinge on its industrial growth.

How then did these divergent perspectives and objectives play out around the negotiating table in Copenhagen?

Before delving into any of the substantive issues of the deliberations, consider for a moment some of the negotiating stagecraft employed by the Chinese. At one of the most critical negotiating sessions, involving key leaders, U.S. President Obama sat next to British Prime Minister Brown, with UN Secretary General Ban Ki Moon a few seats down, and a number of other heads of government gathered in the room. And sitting directly across the negotiating table from Obama was not the Chinese Premier, but rather an anonymous second tier Foreign Ministry official. In the highly choreographed, highly status-conscious world of diplomatic protocol, it would be hard to imagine a more blatant snub. As the negotiations unfolded, Obama and the other heads of government were frequently left waiting, as the lower level Chinese delegate would excuse himself to place phone calls to his superiors.[74]

China's aversion to specifics was so strong that it even pressed to have numerical targets for developed countries removed from the text. A reference to 2020 as the year in which global emissions should peak was changed instead to "as soon as possible."[75]

China's interventions and objections, which in the view of some participants bordered on outright obstructionism, helped to ensure that numerical targets and specific time frames

---

[74] Mark Lynas, "How do I know China wrecked the Copenhagen deal? I was in the room", guardian.co.uk, December 22, 2009,http;//www.guardian.co.uk/environment/2009/dec/22/copenhagen-climate-change-mark.

[75] "Copenhagen Accord of 18 December 2009". Http://unfccc.int

were largely eliminated from the final text. China's positions were frequently backed by certain African nations that have benefited mightily from Chinese investment and development assistance.

The resulting final document was widely condemned as a failure – too vague and non-committal to have any real meaning or impact. There were no legally binding commitments for reducing CO_2 emissions, and the document itself was not even formally adopted, rather it was only "noted". The document was certainly far less than President Obama had hoped to secure through his personal efforts at diplomacy and persuasion. But, it was a document which suited China's national interests and objectives quite well.[76]

The Copenhagen conference can largely be seen as a reflection of Chinese skill and effectiveness in "working" international forums to secure its national interests, and its ability to deflect Western positions, irrespective of how vigorously they are pursued -- or how high-level the interlocutor is -- up to and including the President of the United States.

Chinese Premier Wen Confers with his colleagues from Africa in Copenhagen

---

[76] Peter Browne, "China's Copenhagen Paradox", Inside Story, January 14, 2010, http://inside.org.au/chinas-copenhagen-paradox/

China and Peacekeeping: a Gradual Evolution

The motivation and commitment behind China's participation in United Nations peacekeeping operations have evolved in recent years. When the PRC took over the permanent China seat in the UN Security Council in 1971 as it assumed control of Chinese membership in the UN, Beijing continued its general and strong opposition to peacekeeping operations. This policy was based on China's determined adherence to the traditional doctrine of state sovereignty and independence, and the principle of non-interference in the internal affairs of countries, long cornerstones of Chinese foreign policy. It was also driven by China's experience in the Korean War and the perception in China that the UN was a platform for the United States and the Soviet Union to play out their Cold War battles and struggles for influence.

China's attitude towards peacekeeping changed in the early 1980s in line with Deng Xiaoping's economic and political reforms that started a shift from an ideology-driven foreign policy to a more pragmatic approach.[77] Beijing began to revise the way it perceived the UN and how it participated in the organization and indeed in other institutions and mechanisms of global governance of which it was a part.

In 1981, China cast a vote in the UN Security Council in support of a resolution to authorize the extension of the United Nations Peacekeeping Force in Cyprus (UNFICYP). In explaining China's position, the Chinese representative said that his country's change in policy reflected the shifts in international geopolitics and the "evolution of the role of UN peacekeeping operations." He declared that "from now on, the Chinese government will actively consider and support such UN peacekeeping operations as are conducive to the maintenance of international peace and security and to the preservation of the sovereignty and independence of the states concerned in strict conformity with the purposes and principles of the [UN] Charter."[78]

---

[77] Documents of the Twelfth National Congress of the Communist Party of China, Joint Publishing Company Ltd, Hong Kong, 1982.

[78] United Nations, Meeting Record, S/PV.2313, December 14, 1981.

The next year, China began making financial contributions to support UN peacekeeping. Beijing also set a mission to the Middle East to study peacekeeping operations in the region.[79] China also began to elaborate on the thinking behind its Security Council voting, explaining why it would abstain on votes relating to peacekeeping. It stressed that abstention was a way to cooperate with the international community by acquiescence.

By 1988, China was ready to take its participation and commitment to peacekeeping to a higher level. It became a member of the UN General Assembly committee on peacekeeping operations. A year later, 20 Chinese civilian observers were part of the UN Transition Assistance Group (UNTAG) mission that went to Namibia to monitor elections in that southwestern African country. China's participation in UN peacekeeping expanded quickly after that. In 1990, Chinese military observers joined the UN Truce Supervision Organization (UNTSO) in the Middle East. This marked the first time that China participated officially in UN peacekeeping. Throughout the 1990s and into the next decade, China consistently supported or joined UN peacekeeping operations. In 1991, China was part of a UN peacekeeping operation in the Western Sahara. In 1992 and 1993, China participated in the UN Transitional Authority in Cambodia (UNTAC), providing both financial and political support. It also sent two units of engineers from the People's Liberation Army (PLA). Mozambique and Liberia followed in 1993; Sierra Leone in 1998 and 1999; Ethiopia, Eritrea and Timor Leste in 2000; the Democratic Republic of Congo and Bosnia and Herzegovina in 2001; Liberia again in 2003; Burundi, Côte d'Ivoire, Afghanistan, Kosovo and Haiti in 2004; Sudan in 2005; Lebanon in 2006; Chad and the Central African Republic in 2007; and Haiti after the earthquake in early 2010.[80]

In an indication of how far China had moved in its perception of the peacekeeping role of the UN, the Deputy Chief of the PLA General Staff was reported by the official Xinhua news agency as saying in 2006 that "China is a peace-loving country. In addressing grave issues involving international peace and security, we are a responsible country. Peacekeeping is our mission, and it is also our fundamental principle... Chinese peacekeeping activities demonstrate our country's image as a responsible superpower. The quality of our troops is highly praised by international organizations and other countries, [and] in the course of our peacekeeping activities under the UN Charter, China sets a glorious example."[81]

In the year 2000, China had fewer than 100 people involved in peacekeeping operations. This had risen to 2,137 by the end of February 2010, putting China 14th on the list of top contributors of uniformed personnel to UN peacekeeping operations, just behind Senegal (2,248) and ahead of South Africa

---

[79] International Crisis Group, "China's Growing Role in UN Peacekeeping", Asia Report No. 166, April 17, 2009.

[80] Ibid.

[81] Major General Zhang Qinsheng, interview with Xinhua News Agency, September 28, 2006, as quoted in Bonny Ling, " China's Peacekeeping Diplomacy", China Rights Forum, Human Rights in China, No. 1, 2007.

(1,973). The top five countries on the list: Bangladesh (10,852), Pakistan (10,733), India (8,783), Nigeria (5,837), and Egypt (5,258). China leads the five permanent members of the Security Council. France ran second among the so-called P5 and 16th overall, with 1,673 peacekeepers. None of the other P5 nations were in the top 20.[82] Over more than two decades, China has sent about 15,000 people to participate in some 18 UN peacekeeping missions and is currently part of nine of 15 ongoing operations. Early this year, China sent fresh contingents of peacekeepers to Timor Leste (its 15th deployment since 2000) and Sudan.[83]

In terms of personnel, China and other emerging countries have clearly filled in a void left in recent years by the diminishing participation of developed nations, particularly the P5. But developed countries remain the chief financial supporters of UN peacekeeping operations. As of the end of February 2010, the top five contributors to the UN peacekeeping budget were the US (21.17%), Japan (12.53%), the United Kingdom (8.16%), Germany (8.02%) and France (7.56%). China, however, was not too far behind, ranked 7th, with 3.94% of the budget, behind Italy (5%) and ahead of Canada (3.21%), Spain (3.18%), the Republic of Korea (2.26%) and Russia (1.98%).[84]

China's commitment to peacekeeping has remained consistent in recent years, despite tragedies such as the death in 2006 of a soldier involved in Lebanon. Two months later, China increased its troop strength in Lebanon, making its group there the biggest that it has had in any peacekeeping operation.[85] While the death of eight Chinese peacekeepers in the earthquake in Haiti in January 2010 was a wrenching moment for the nation, China continued its participation in the peacekeeping operation in the Caribbean country, sending replacements just days later.[86]

From China's perspective, its motivation for joining peacekeeping operations is a manifestation of its increasing responsiveness to growing international expectations as a result of its emergence as a major economic and geopolitical power in Asia and the world, and its desire to enhance its credibility and exert more influence with the UN.

Along the way, China has discovered or at least grown to appreciate that participating in peacekeeping provides other benefits. First, there are clear military benefits. The PLA's long focus on national security

---

[82] United Nations Department of Peacekeeping Operations, Fact Sheet, "United Nations Peacekeeping", March, 2010

[83] "15th Chinese Peacekeeping Force deploys in East Timor for rotation duty", People's Daily, May 12, 2010.

[84] United Nations Department of Peacekeeping Operations, Fact Sheet, "United Nations Peacekeeping", March, 2010

[85] "China ups Lebanon force to 1,000", BBC News, September 18, 2006.

[86] "Chinese Peacekeeping reinforcements arrive in Haiti", Xinhua News Agency, January 26, 2010.

and specifically the potential for conflict across the Taiwan Strait has defined it as a state institution. The PLA has been primed for war in the event that China's national sovereignty and the One China ideal would somehow be under threat. But as China has evolved into a modern nation and major power, its political and military leadership have come to see the need to transform its armed forces into a modern institution for the 21st Century.

Peacekeeping has opened new missions for the PLA. It has created opportunities for the PLA to foster closer cooperation with other military forces around the world, including many of its major security partners. Participation in peacekeeping operations including counter-piracy efforts to protect Chinese merchant vessels off Somalia, disaster response and humanitarian relief has also allowed the PLA to assess its own capacities, strengths and weaknesses against those of other militaries. Chinese military personnel, for example, have had access to and learned about using such technology as GPS. Peacekeeping operations have provided Chinese troops – both army and police – and civilian personnel valuable experience, expanding their knowledge, outlook and capabilities at home and abroad. Participation in nation-building efforts – the "blue-beret" missions – have also helped Chinese peacekeepers acquire and develop soft-power tools and experience that would be useful for China's diplomacy, particularly in regions critical to its interests such as Africa and Southeast Asia.

At this point, however, China's commitment to peacekeeping is complicated by the constraints it faces, given its continuing adherence to the traditional view of state sovereignty and the principle of non-interference. The international community's expectations for China's participation or support of peacekeeping, particularly in test-case countries or regions such as the Sudan, should not rise too high. But it is similarly unrealistic to portray China's position on sovereignty today as entirely rigid. There is a discernible gap between China's rhetoric in robust defense of the traditional concept of sovereignty – motivated in large part by its concern that the international community may interfere in its domestic affairs, notably the Taiwan and Tibet situations – and where it seems to be, given its actual behavior.

Indeed, China will continue to judge whether to support a peacekeeping operation on a case-by-case basis. Instinctively, the traditional view of state sovereignty and non-interference will prevail. Yet China has on record endorsed at least twice the concept of the responsibility to protect (R2P), which essentially redefines sovereignty as the responsibility to protect its citizens from mass atrocities such as genocide, war crimes, ethnic cleansing and crimes against humanity. While China harbored some suspicions that R2P could be an instrument that Western nations could use to interfere in the internal affairs of countries they accuse of human-rights abuses, it supported the UN's unanimous endorsement of the R2P principle at the 2005 World Summit in New York, reiterating its stance in a position paper on UN reform that stated: "When a massive humanitarian crisis occurs, it is the legitimate concern of the international community to ease and defuse the crisis."[87]

---

[87] "Position Paper of the People's Republic of China on the United Nations Reforms", Beijing, June 7, 2005, quoted in Ramesh Thakur, The United Nations, Peace and Security, Cambridge University Press, 2006.

Soon after that landmark UN endorsement, then-Secretary General Kofi Annan sought Security Council action to bolster the General Assembly's decision. Algeria, China and Russia initially did not support a resolution. But negotiations convinced China to change its position when it was agreed to use in the Security Council resolution the same language employed in the World Summit endorsement document. China's switch put pressure on the other holdouts. In April 2006 – with China presiding over the Security Council session – Resolution 1674 was approved unanimously, boosting the R2P cause.

As soon as Resolution 1674 was passed, China was careful to downplay its significance, casting it as simply a restatement of the World Summit endorsement of R2P, which applied strictly to genocide, war crimes, ethnic cleansing, and crimes against humanity. Beijing warned strongly against the inappropriate expansion of the interpretation and application of R2P. In a 2007 Security Council debate, Chinese ambassador Liu Zhenmin stressed that, while governments did have the responsibility to protect civilians, "even when outside support is necessary, the will of the country concerned must be fully respected and forcible intervention avoided." The Security Council, Liu added, "should not be the forum for extrapolating this concept or engaging in similar legislative activities."[88]

This has essentially remained China's position, supporting the important role that the Security Council and other parts of the UN and the international community have in preventing armed conflict, mitigating its effects and protecting civilians. For China, prevention is what is critical. Intervention must be undertaken only within the very specific boundaries set in the UN's R2P endorsement. From its perspective, non-interference remains a core principle. But it has, at the same time, articulated that the international community has a special responsibility and moral obligation to address peace and security problems in Africa and must explore global, regional and national approaches to do so.

Yet even as China has held on to this position, it has continued to develop its peacekeeping commitments. In 2007, the PLA held an unprecedented internal meeting on peacekeeping, involving senior officials from government, the public security apparatus and the military. Senior military officials at an international security seminary organized by the PLA in 2007 supported increasing China's participation in peacekeeping operations, humanitarian relief, counter-terrorism exercises and post-conflict reconstruction initiatives. China launched a new peacekeeping training center in 2009, its third such facility.[89] (The United Kingdom has provided some support to China for peacekeeper training, including English-language study.) In August 2007, a Chinese general was named the force commander

---

[88] Statement by H.E. Ambassador LIU Zhenmin at the Open Debate of the Security Council on 'Protection of Civilians in Armed Conflicts", Permanent Mission of the People's Republic of China to the UN, November 20, 2007.

[89] Bates Gill and Chin-Hao Huang, "China spreads its peacekeepers", Asia Times Online, February 4, 2009.

of the UN Mission for the Referendum in Western Sahara (MINURSO), the first time that a Chinese citizen had filled such a position.[90]

Indeed, since 2000, China has been consistent in supporting peacekeeping operations even if a mission is empowered by the UN to use force and may be deeply involved in the reconstruction and administration of the host state. China has also called for greater transparency in peacekeeping operations to ensure that resources are allocated where the needs are greatest. It has also pushed for strengthening the UN Peace-building Commission and for better coordination with regional organizations such as the African Union.

China in Africa

Consider the case of the Sudan, which is widely referred to by China's critics as a case where Beijing has sought to protect the government of the host state out of concerns for Chinese commercial interests, specifically its access to oil resources. It is not lost on observers of China's peacekeeping participation that three quarters of the missions of which it is a part are in Africa, a region in which China has been making major trade and investment inroads in recent years, sometimes with great controversy.

The Sudan is the prime example. China is a major economic partner of the country, investing in the domestic oil industry and also providing technical assistance and supplying small arms and weapons. But criticism that China has sought to impede UN efforts to resolve the Darfur problem or shield the Sudanese government should be somewhat tempered. There is some evidence that, in the case of Darfur, China has supported efforts at a political reconciliation and the deployment of an African Union-UN peacekeeping force to resolve the humanitarian crisis. In 2008, China practically doubled its deployment of military engineers in Darfur, signaling that it was prepared to support the larger force called for by many in the international community. In mid-July 2010, it sent another contingent, including 220 police officers to the Sudan.[91]

Despite what was seen as China's resistance to Security Council action on Darfur, China has arguably demonstrated that it can play a constructive role, at least in some respects. Wang Guangya, Chinese Ambassador to the UN, played a critical role in the November 2006 talks in Addis Ababa that resulted in a plan for the deployment of UN peacekeepers in Darfur. China has also supported de-mining operations in the region and mechanisms for controlling weapons. It has also provided financial support for African Union and UN mediation. While it was seen as a public relations measure, Beijing's appointment of a

---

[90] United Nations Mission for the Referendum in Western Sahara (MINURSO), "Press release", Laayoune, September 17, 2007.

[91] "First echelon of 7th Chinese peacekeeping force to Sudan sets out", People's Liberation Army Daily, July 19, 2010.

special envoy for Darfur, who is reported to have channeled blunt messages to the Sudanese government, was further evidence of China's evolving approach.

Myanmar is another case in point. China also has strong commercial ties with Myanmar and is interested in accessing the country's natural resources. While China has impeded Security Council resolutions relating to the Southeast Asian nation, it has played a vital role in pushing the military leadership to continue its dialogue with UN officials. While it opposed international military intervention to circumvent Myanmar's refusal of assistance after the cyclone disaster in 2008, China was quick to provide aid and relief to the country.

While China has not come nearly as far as its critics in the United States and elsewhere would like to see, and while some of its actions are more cosmetic than substantive, it does need to be acknowledged that there has been some movement. This is one of those areas in which China's increasing engagement in international institutions has been, at least is some modest respects, a two-way street.

In considering the thinking behind China's participation in peacekeeping operations, it is also important to consider the impact of the Taiwan situation on its strategy. Since taking over the UN China seat in 1971, Beijing has been engaged in a long-running battle with Taipei over diplomatic space. This fight for influence intensified in the 1990s and took on even greater urgency in 2000 once Chen Shui-bian of the pro-independence Democratic Progressive Party became the president of Taiwan. There is no doubt that China sees the inroads it has made in Africa as aiding its efforts to isolate Taiwan. China's motives for building trade and investment ties in the continent are mainly commercial – it needs access to vital natural resources – but pushing Taiwan out is obviously regarded as a positive "side effect."

Taiwan has formal diplomatic ties with four African countries (Burkina Faso, Gambia, Sao Tome and Principe, and Swaziland), six states in the Pacific (Kiribati, Marshall Islands, Nauru, Palau, Solomon Islands and Tuvalu), 12 nations in the Americas including the Caribbean (Belize, Dominican Republic, El Salvador, Guatemala, Haiti, Honduras, Nicaragua, Panama, Paraguay, Saint Kitts and Nevis, Saint Lucia, and Saint Vincent and the Grenadines), and one European state (the Holy See).[92]

China found that not just participation in peacekeeping but also development assistance in general could be a powerful tool for persuading countries to switch recognition. Liberia did so in 2003 just before China sent PLA troops to the country to help with water projects. China also provided aid to Liberia, including food, motorcycles for its police, and a sports complex.

In 1996, after Taiwan's vice-president was invited to the inauguration of Haiti's president, China took steps to delay the deployment of a peacekeeping force to the Caribbean country for several weeks. A year later, following Guatemala's recognition of Taiwan, China vetoed a proposed peacekeeping mission

---

[92] Ministry of Foreign Affairs, Republic of China (Taiwan), "Diplomatic Allies",
http://www.moga.gov.tw/webapp/ct.asp?xltem=32618&CtNode=1379&mp=6

to the region, but later lifted its objections. The Kosovo crisis in 1998-1999 presented a particular quandary for China because of the Yugoslav Federation's assertion that it would not permit Kosovo to break away from Serbia. The parallels with Taiwan were obvious. The bombing of the Chinese embassy in Belgrade hardened China's objections to Security Council-approved military intervention. But by 2004, China's position had changed and it sent a 12-strong police contingent to join the United Nations Mission in Kosovo (UNMIK).[93]

The clearest example of Taiwan being a factor in China's decision whether to support peacekeeping in a particular country was in the case of the Former Yugoslav Republic of Macedonia. In 1999, two weeks after Skopje established ties with Taipei, which had dangled US$1 billion in investment as enticement, China vetoed the extension of the UN peacekeeping mandate in the Balkan country. Security Council members condemned the vote, which China denied was linked to Taiwan's diplomatic success. Within months, in part due to shifts in the country's domestic politics, Macedonia reverted to recognizing Beijing.[94]

While its UN veto may have contributed to inducing Skopje back to its side, China was clearly chastened by the Macedonia episode. Beijing has since moderated its strategy in tandem with its more nuanced approach to Taiwan. In 2004, China's support and participation in the UN Stabilization Mission in Haiti (MINUSTAH) was the first time Beijing joined peacekeeping operations in a host country with which it did not have formal diplomatic relations.[95] The deaths of the eight Chinese peacekeepers in the Haiti earthquake in January 2010 were therefore particularly poignant because they occurred in a country that has steadfastly maintained recognition of Taiwan. China was among the first nations to respond to the earthquake, sending rescue personnel, aid and supplies. Beijing was sensitive to criticism that, once the bodies of its police delegation had been recovered, it had withdrawn from the country. In fact, China had maintained medical personnel in Haiti and sent some replacements for the peacekeepers who had died.

The tragedy in Haiti became a major domestic issue in China, generating debate over the merits of the police. It also raised questions about the diplomatic competition with Taiwan, which had cooled with the election of Ma Ying-jeou of the Kuomintang to succeed Chen Shui-bian as president. Ma has focused more on cross-strait rapprochement. His approach yielded a major concession from Beijing which lifted its objection to Taiwan attending the World Health Assembly as an observer, essentially gaining observer status in the World Health Organization (WHO), something that Taipei had been seeking for years, especially after the SARS outbreak in 2003. After the Haiti earthquake, Taiwan also sent a mission

---

[93] Antoaneta Bezlova, "Kosovo Holds Lesson for Tibet, Taiwan", Inter Press Service (IPS) News Agency, February 19, 2008.

[94] Alexander Casella, "Macedonia: Taiwan's Lost Gambit", *Asia Times Online*, July 11, 2001.

[95] China Confirms Deaths of all 8 Chinese Police Officers in Haiti Quake". Xinhua, January 17, 2010

and Ma even met the Haitian prime minister during a transit stop in Santo Domingo, the capital of the Dominican Republic.

It is a testament to the greater sophistication of Chinese diplomacy and foreign policy that Taiwan's aggressive efforts in Haiti after the earthquake, which dwarfed China's contributions in value, did not cause much consternation in Beijing. Certainly, China could not be seen as being upset at a time of extreme calamity in Haiti, no matter that the country is in Taipei's camp. Commentators suggest that the Haiti episode has further strengthened the argument in Beijing that it should focus on economic diplomacy and not let politics including the Taiwan factor interfere overtly in peacekeeping and humanitarian efforts.

Indeed, Beijing seems poised to develop further its peacekeeping capacity. In late July 2010, at a reception to commemorate the 83rd anniversary of the founding of the PLA and 20 years of China's participation in UN peacekeeping operations, the UN peacekeeping chief Alain Le Roy lauded China for its support. Chinese peacekeepers have displayed "a great degree of professionalism, discipline and dedication," he said. They are doing "a fantastic job."[96]

Earlier the same month, the deputy director of the peacekeeping affairs office at the Ministry of National Defense said that China would consider sending combat troops on missions if requested by the UN. (China's deployment to Timor Leste in 2000 was the first time that Chinese police officers were authorized to carry pistols and conduct patrols.)[97]

So far, no such request has been received, but if one were made, China would consider it with extreme caution. This echoed similar comments made by other officials, and could signal that China is prepared to take its participation in UN peacekeeping operations to yet another level. For now, its peacekeepers are mainly engineers, medics, and transport and logistics specialists.

Constructive Contributions, Tactical Benefits

China rightfully deserves credit for its contributions to UN peacekeeping missions, both in terms of financial and manpower support. The loss of life amongst Chinese military personnel in defense of UN principles is no less heroic and no less painful than the loss of American military personnel under similar circumstances.

---

[96] "UN official lauds China's peacekeeping efforts" Xinhua News Agency, July 30, 2010.

[97] Yin He, "The peacekeeping dragon is on safari", Asia Times Online, February 8, 2008, and "Timor police to carry guns", BBC News, February 10, 2000.

At the same time, it should be noted that China's peacekeeping activities have also been wise from a tactical point of view, undercutting some of its critics, obtaining useful military expertise, and expanding its credibility and clout within the UN. China's conduct in peacekeeping (and the UN in general) also serves to illustrate China's skill in utilizing international institutions to put down clear markers on the Taiwan issue, although as was seen in the case of Haiti, this approach seems to be loosening.

Case Study

China in Haiti:

Paying a heavy price to keep the peace and support the UN

As one of the most dysfunctional states in the Western Hemisphere, Haiti has long relied on UN support for many of its basic needs. With an extremely weak police force, and no armed forces of its own, Haiti has turned to UN peacekeepers to maintain security, order, and stability in the country.

Despite Haiti's recognition of Taiwan, and the attendant lack of official diplomatic relations with the PRC, China began participating in UN peacekeeping operations in Haiti in October of 2004. This represented the first time China supported peacekeeping operations in a country that maintains diplomatic recognition of Taiwan. Several factors could potentially explain this, including a desire to enhance its international reputation, a belief that an incentive-based approach rather than a heavy-handed approach would yield better results, and/or that a future Haitian government that might ultimately emerge from the current disorder would be more favorably predisposed towards China as a result of its supportive peacekeeping efforts[98]. Some combination of these factors, along with a degree of genuine humanitarian concern, probably provide the most credible explanation.

In any case, Chinese peacekeepers in Haiti serve as either civil police or riot police, and engage in activities such as patrol, vehicle inspection, emergency response, and special tasks such as hostage rescue.

At the time of Haiti earthquake in January of this year, a total of 142 Chinese peacekeepers were serving in country. Eight of these soldiers were called to a meeting with UN officials in Port-au-Prince on the fateful morning of the quake, and lost their lives when the building collapsed.[99]

Days later, one of the first foreign support teams to arrive in Haiti was from China, consisting of more than 60 personnel and carrying 10 tons of food, equipment, and medicine. A second

[98] International Crisis Group, "China's Growing Role in UN Peacekeeping", Asia Report No. 166, April 17, 2009.

[99] "China Confirms Deaths of all 8 Chinese Police Officers in Haiti Quake". Xinhua, January 17, 2010.

team would arrive roughly two weeks later, with 40 military medical professionals who rendered care and treatment to over 4000 Haitians. The eight peacekeepers who were lost were eventually replaced.

As has been pointed out elsewhere, China does receive some important reputational and even operational benefits from its support of UN peacekeeping. However, the same could be said for virtually any other country that supports peacekeeping operations (including the United States). This should not be allowed to obscure the reality that China's participation does constitute a very real and very constructive contribution to the UN system, and international humanitarian efforts. As was identified in the ten trends in the introduction, in at least some respects China is becoming a valued and constructive member of the international system, and in cases like the Haiti earthquake they have paid a heavy price for their support.

Chinese peacekeeping police salute a vehicle carrying the last of their deceased colleagues in Port-au-Prince, capital of Haiti, on Jan. 16, 2010.

The Asian Development Bank (ADB)

The evolution of China's role within the ADB provides an interesting window into a number of patterns and behaviors which can tell us much about China's approach to international institutions overall. As with several other organizations under review, China is extremely effective in tapping into the technical expertise that is available through the ADB. China is also, in at least some respects, an increasingly mature and constructive institutional member of the ADB. And perhaps most strikingly, China has grown quite assertive (some would say almost combative) within the ADB in protecting and promoting what it views as its national interests on geo-strategic and political matters.

A Major Contretemps over India

The normally placid inner-workings of the ADB received a sharp jolt in 2009 as China responded in decidedly undiplomatic and assertive terms (at least by ADB standards) to what it viewed as an unacceptable foray into a "political" matter involving the country partnership strategy for India.

Typically, approval of ADB country partnership strategies, which outline multiyear plans for development projects, rarely create controversy within the bank, and it is rarer still for these plans to actually be blocked or postponed. China however did in fact block approval of the country plan for India because it included funding for a project in a disputed territory.[100]

Since 1962 when the two countries fought a brief war over the issue, India and China have been locked in a territorial dispute over Arunachal Pradesh, a largely uninhabitable Himalayan region. In recent years, China has grown more strident on the issue.

The 3 year, $2.9 billion ADB country partnership program for India which was to go before the Board included $60 million for a flood management program in the disputed territory. The official and public response of China was quick and unequivocal,[101] as expressed by a Foreign Ministry spokesman:

"The Asian Development Bank, regardless of the major concerns of China, approved the India country partnership strategy which involves the territorial dispute between China and India... China expresses its strong dissatisfaction over this. The Bank's move not only seriously tarnishes its own name, but also undermines the interests of its members."[102]

---

[100] Minder, Raphael, "China blocks ADB India loan plan". Financial Times, April 10, 2009.

[101] Ibid.

[102] "China Slams ADB Over India Funding." Sina.com. June 19, 2009
http://english.sina.com/china/2009/0618/249531.html.

The same statement went on to reassert China's "non-interference" doctrine: "The Asian Development Bank, as a regional development institution should not interfere in the political affairs of the members. The Chinese government strongly urges the Asian Development Bank to take effective measures to eliminate the negative impact of this move".[103]

In the context of the normally non-controversial administration of the ADB country aid programs, the combativeness of the Chinese response was unprecedented. According to one Bank official, "The ADB has never deferred any loan to India. There is nothing like that in the past."[104]

And in the mind of some observers, the dispute over the India project raises larger questions about the overall arc of China's growing assertiveness not only within the ADB, but in multilateral institutions more broadly. According to the *Financial Times* of London:

"China's reluctance to approve the country plan for India comes at a time when Beijing is lobbying hard for a larger role in the International Monetary Fund and other international organizations... this incident could herald future conflicts once China gains the influence it is seeking in multilateral organizations if future initiatives infringe on what China sees as its interests.... Some analysts also worry that greater Chinese involvement in institutions such as the IMF could allow it to wield veto powers over rescue packages for countries that that did not comply with its political demands, especially over issues such as Tibet and Taiwan" [105]

Later in 2009, in response to China's strong protestations, the ADB acquiesced and decided to implement the projects in its India development plan "one by one in an effort to prevent a territorial dispute with China disrupting one of its biggest lending programs".[106]

While this move effectively bought time and calmed the waters, some were still taken aback at China's forcefulness. ADB Director-General Rajat Nag expressed surprise at China's hard line stance on the issue, and Indian Prime Minister Manmohan Singh also expressed a certain incomprehension over the Chinese approach. Speaking at the Council of Foreign Relations, Singh commented that "... we also recognize that we have a long-standing border problem with China. We are trying to resolve it through dialogue... But there is a certain amount of assertiveness on the part of the Chinese. I don't fully understand the reasons for it." [107]

---

[103] "China Slams ADB Over India Funding." Sina.com. June 19, 2009
http://english.sina.com/china/2009/0618/249531.html.

[104] Minder, Raphael, "China blocks ADB India loan plan". Financial Times, April 10, 2009

[105] Ibid.

[106] Lamont, James. "ADB Adopts Piecemeal Strategy In India After Chinese Objections." Financial Times. 28 November 28, 2009 , http://www.ft.com/cms/s/0/57d88396-dbbd-11de-9424-00144feabdc0.html

[107] Lamont, James. "ADB Adopts Piecemeal Strategy In India After Chinese Objections." Financial Times. November 28, 2009 , http://www.ft.com/cms/s/0/57d88396-dbbd-11de-9424-00144feabdc0.html

His public comments notwithstanding, Prime Minister Singh probably does in fact understand the reasons for China's assertiveness. Symbolic gestures – and the underlying power-plays they represent – are important to the Chinese. The ADB and other multilateral institutions provide China with a high-profile stage to on which to make these symbolic power-plays, and are a subtle but effective means to lay down strategic markers, flex muscles, and gain tacit, if not explicit, acceptance of the Chinese viewpoint.

An Active and Engaged Institutional Member

Alongside its rising assertiveness, China has also grown to be a mature and actively engaged member of the ADB, both in terms of what it contributes to, and extracts from, the organization.

For instance, the Bank of China (BoC) -- the largest trade financing bank, and one of the four leading commercial banks in the PRC -- is now focused on transforming itself into a world-class financial institution. It is aggressively availing itself of a number of ADB programs to support that objective. The ADB has provided training to BoC staff under the Trade Finance Facilitation Program, and since 2006 the ADB has conducted 5 technical assistance projects encompassing corporate governance, environmental safeguards, anti-money laundering, anti-corruption, and operational risk management. In July of this year, the ADB and the BoC agreed to explore collaboration in regional trade finance, clean energy and infrastructure development, microfinance and institutional capacity building. A regular staff exchange program is also expected to begin later this year, providing an opportunity to further professionalize BoC staff.[108]

The East Asia section of the ADB produces the largest number of publications within the Bank, and the lion's share of these result from Chinese requests. The Chinese ministry of Finance has requested knowledge products from the ADB on a range of issues, including topics such as property markets and the formation of asset bubbles. And, in the aftermath of the tragic Sichuan earthquake, China tapped the ADB's expertise on disaster response management.

As China has grown and developed, its "transactional" relationship with the ADB has also evolved. Since joining the ADB in 1986 has received a total of $22.96 billion in loans assistance, making it the largest ADB borrower and largest client for private sector financing. But more recently things have been changing and over the past five years, lending to China as a percentage of ADB operations has declined. ADB has directed its support to regions and sectors not benefitting from China's economic boom.[109]

---

[108] "ADB , Bank of China to Broaden Strategic Cooperation." Asian Development Bank, Jul y 13, 2010
http://www.adb.org/Media/printer.asp?articleID=13278

[109] "Asian Development Bank : Overview of Support to China", Asian Development Bank 2010

China is now not only a recipient of ADB loan assistance, but is also a contributor to the Central Asia Regional Economic Cooperation (CAREC) Program and the Greater Mekong Subregional (GMS) Cooperation Program.[110]

Over the course of the past 5-7 years China has taken an increasingly active role in operational issues, and commenting extensively and insightfully on projects entirely unrelated to China. Even those observers prone to be critical of China for other aspects of its conduct concede that China does its "homework," is well prepared, and constructive in these respects. China is also increasingly positioning itself during Board and other deliberations as somewhat of a model for the developing country members, although by most accounts it does not presume or attempt to speak for the developing world.

---

[110] Asian Development Bank website: www.adb.org

CASE STUDY

China: A Responsible Stakeholder?

In 2005, then-Deputy Secretary of State Robert Zoellick gave a speech that came to be known as the "Responsible Stakeholder" speech. It attracted a good deal of attention in the United States, China, and other countries around the world at the time, and is still instructive to review today.

In his remarks, Zoellick essentially called on China – as a country that had transformed itself largely as a result of its participation in the international system – to now take on a greater leadership for that system. In Zoellick's words:

"All nations conduct diplomacy to promote their national interests. Responsible stakeholders go further: They recognize that the international system sustains their peaceful prosperity, so they work to sustain that system… As a responsible stakeholder, China would be more than just a member – it would work with us to sustain the international system that has enabled its success."[111]

Zoellick went on to walk through a number of troublesome issues, and outlined how China could and should behave differently if it was in fact a responsible stakeholder. We now have more than 5 years of perspective and historical record since those remarks were made, and what is perhaps most striking as one revisits those various issues, is how little has changed. Although China's role and stake in the international system has only increased in the intervening 5 years, there has been little appreciable evidence that they have accepted the Zoellick argument on being a responsible stakeholder.

In a reference to China's commercial relationships in Africa and elsewhere in the developing world, Zoellick said: "China is acting as if it can somehow "lock up" energy supplies around the world. This is not a sensible path to achieving energy security. Moreover, a mercantilist strategy leads to partnerships with regimes that hurt China's reputation and lead others to question its intentions". Zoellick called on China to work cooperatively with the United States on market strategies that would lessen volatility, instability, and hoarding.

---

[111] All references to speech taken from: Zoellick, Robert. "Whither China: From Membership to Responsibility" Speech, September 21, 2005.

Since that time however, China has only proved to more adept and proactive in forging relationships in Africa and elsewhere with dubious regimes, in order to provide greater and more secure access to energy supplies.

Zoellick reckoned that "China should take more than oil from Sudan – it should take some responsibility for resolving Sudan's human crisis."

Despite any symbolic or behind the scenes efforts China might have made in Africa, the fact remains that it has not played anywhere near the constructive role that Zoellick called for.

Zoellick also called on China to do more to ease tensions with North Korea. The sinking of the South Korean naval ship Cheonan, the shelling of Yeonpyeong Island, as well as the seemingly never-ending stand-off over North Korea's nuclear program and proliferation practices provide China with ample opportunity to play a constructive role. But all of China's actions or inactions have served to simply demonstrate that the overriding Chinese interest on the Korean peninsula is to prevent any increased pressure on the North Korean regime that could potentially lead to an implosion, and the resulting massive out-migration of impoverished North Koreans across the border into China.

Zoellick of course also attempted to nudge China on its massive trade surplus and mercantilist practices, saying that no country "would accept a $162 billion trade deficit." In the years since that remark, however, the US trade deficit with China has only increased, and now stands at $227 billion.[112]

On the issue of IPR, Zoellick opined that "a responsible major player shouldn't tolerate rampant theft of intellectual property and counterfeiting..." As anyone who has had recent experience in the bustling DVD markets of Beijing can readily attest, this notion does not seem to have been even partially embraced, and senior executives at several large US corporations have recently stepped up their criticism of China's intellectual property rights (IPR) practices, in particular the "indigenous innovation policy" which use government procurement and other policies to force technology transfer, and otherwise violate IPR. China has demonstrated unambiguously over the years that its approach to IPR has less to do with protecting the products and profits of non-Chinese companies, and more to do with the ways in which IPR policy can be used to support the development of Chinese industry -- a clear rebuke to the type of fundamental change called for by Mr. Zoellick.

---

[112] Office of the United States Trade Representative website. Http://www.ustr.gov/countries-regions/china

On the issue of the exchange rate, Zoellick said: "China's recent policy adjustments are an initial step, but much more remains to be done ..." So little has changed on the exchange rate issue that this very same line could be inserted into a speech to be delivered tomorrow by the U.S. Treasury Secretary and it would not seem inappropriate or out of place. In the view of most credible economic analysis the RMB continues to be undervalued by as much as 20-40 percent.

The strategy of calling on China to act as a responsible stakeholder has failed to elicit significant changes in China's policies for two reasons: first, it is based on a questionable premise; and second, it fails to sufficiently grasp the Chinese perspective.

This strategy is based on the dubious premise that China believes it is in its interests to strengthen and support the existing US-lead framework in the current international system. The appeal of acting as somewhat of a "supporting partner" in what is seen as a U.S.-dominated game is questionable at best.

There is also a good deal of skepticism within Chinese policy circles, and a suspicion that U.S. admonishments for China to be a responsible stakeholder have considerably less to do with a genuine US concern for the commonweal of the international community, and more to do with buttressing the U.S. position of preeminence within that system.

And finally, it must also be pointed out that, from the Chinese perspective, there is also somewhat of a condensing tone in these admonishments. The implication is that China is somehow behaving irresponsibly if it fails to follow strictures annunciated by the United States. Chinese officials, who have to confront on a daily basis the reality of hundreds of millions of China's citizens living at, or just above, the poverty level, might have very different definitions about what it means to act "responsibly."

A Brief Look at Lower Impact Institutions

As was mentioned in the introduction, some institutions and organizations wield greater global influence than others, and the variation in the relative impact of the organizations under review is reflected in the depth of the treatment provided to each.

There are several additional lower impact institutions or organizations which, although they lack the global relevance of the UN or the World Bank, are still worth briefly reviewing because they can underline important trends, and/or hold the potential to take on greater importance in the years to come.

The Shanghai Cooperation Council

Long on ambition but short on concrete accomplishments, the Shanghai Cooperation Council (SCO) should nonetheless not drop completely off the radar screen of U.S. policy makers. It does have the potential to grow in influence, and exert a more pronounced impact on one or more issues of strategic importance to the United States.

Comprising China, Russia, Kazakhstan, Kyrgyzstan, Tajikistan, and Uzbekistan, the SCO was established in 1996 primarily as a mechanism to resolve border disputes. Although security-related issues are ostensibly paramount, the SCO's agenda has broadened remarkably, and now includes cultural cooperation, economic issues, foreign affairs, and even banking and financial reform. A longer term objective of the SCO is to establish a free trade area; however, little actual progress towards this objective has been made to date.[113]

Although the SCO charter says that it "is not an alliance directed against other states and regions and it adheres to the principle of openness," it would be difficult not to see the SCO as being at least partially intended to discourage U.S. "meddling" in regions bordering on China and Russia. Indeed, the single SCO initiative which has attracted the most worldwide attention was actually a jab at the regional U.S. military presence. In 2005, the SCO officially called for the United States to establish a timeline for withdrawing all of its military bases from Central Asia. Military cooperation between SCO members is increasing and large-scale war games between China and Russia were held in 2005, 2007, and 2009.[114]

---

[113] Andrew Scheineson, "The Sanghai Cooperation Organization", March 24, 2009, http://www.c fr.org/publication/10883/shanghai_cooperation_organization.html

[114] Ibid.

There are several points worth noting in regard to the SCO. First, it is a China-driven institution which *explicitly excludes* the United States – even as just an observer. The United States formally requested observer status in 2005, but this request was officially declined by the SCO.

Another aspect of the SCO that is noteworthy is its potential significance on energy-related issues. Central Asia is an extremely resource-rich region, containing roughly 20% of the world's proven oil reserves and 45% of the world's proven natural gas reserves, and the SCO has not surprisingly attempted to establish itself as a platform for greater cooperation and collaboration in energy. At an SCO Summit in 2007, Vladimir Putin called for the "creation of an energy club," and at that same meeting member states agreed to establish a "unified energy market" for oil and gas exports, and to promote preferential energy agreements.

Once again though, in concrete terms little has actually happened, and the SCO is unlikely to become an OPEC-like energy cartel anytime soon. This is due in no small part to a lack of cohesion within the group. China and Russia are to one degree or another competing with each other for both energy and influence in the region, and this rivalry has helped frustrate the ambitions of the SCO.

In terms of its relations with other institutions or political groupings, the SCO has established relationships primarily with entities which do not include the United States: the Commonwealth of Independent States, ASEAN, the Organization of Islamic Conference, the EU, and the UN, where it is an observer at the General Assembly. Iran, which currently has observer status at the SCO, has expressed interest in joining the SCO, but thus far the SCO has been cool to Iran's overtures. The likely calculation from Beijing's perspective is that whatever benefits Iranian participation might potentially bring, it would outweighed by the headaches and complications it would cause. This does not suggest, however, that this calculation cannot shift over time.

Although not deeply impactful at the moment, the SCO bears further watching for 3 simple reasons: 1) it draws several energy resource-rich countries into a more formalized sphere of cooperation with Beijing; 2) it has unambiguously rebuffed the U.S. request to become an observer; and 3) its geographic nexus is right on the doorstep of Afghanistan, in a strategically important and politically combustible part of the world.

Irrespective of whether or not the SCO ultimately grows in influence, it does illustrate Beijing's ongoing interest in nurturing institutions with potential geostrategic and economic importance that pointedly do not include the United States, and which are not built upon the same philosophical pillars as the traditional Bretton Woods-style international institutions.

China's involvement with the International Atomic Energy Agency (IAEA) serves to illustrate two of the overall trends identified at the onset: 1) China's tactical shrewdness in "working" the international system; and 2) its laser-like focus on tapping into the international technical expertise available within international organizations. China's approach to the IAEA also provides a good example of one of the identified "truisms": China's strong desire for a stable international environment in which to pursue its economic development.

From a "headline" foreign policy point of view, the issue of greatest impact that involves the IAEA is the development of the nuclear capacity of Iran. On this issue, China has been tactically sophisticated -- and largely successful -- in pursuing its interests.

While the United States has clearly spear-headed international efforts to curb Iran's nuclear ambitions, it must be acknowledged that China would hardly view the prospect of a nuclear-armed Iran as a positive development. Any development that could upset the Middle Eastern geostrategic chess board, raise the prospects for conflict, and potentially threaten the smooth flow of Middle Eastern oil supplies would not be welcomed in stability-conscious Beijing.

China's preference would likely be for some form of a diplomatic solution, but its strong economic interests in Iran (China gets 12% of its oil from Iran, and it has significant financial and trade interests as well) mean that Beijing is unlikely to ever be as ardent as Washington in tightening the screws on Tehran. The possibility of economic sanctions with "real bite" could also end up "biting" China fairly hard.[115]

Given these realities, and the contradictory pressures they imply, a protracted period of "wheel spinning" that never really goes anywhere is probably an acceptable, if not desirable, outcome from the Chinese perspective. Neither a sharply escalated international clamp-down on Iran, consisting of severe sanctions, or in the most extreme case, some form of military action -- nor the reality of a nuclear-armed Iran -- would suit China's interests. An ongoing stand-off that stews on a low simmer without ever boiling over is probably the best realistic short-to-medium term scenario that China can hope for.

China has deftly worked the system to increase the chances for such an outcome. Consider the Chinese approach: Chinese officials have consistently voiced strong support for ongoing diplomatic efforts. Hu Xiaodi, China's permanent representative and ambassador to international organizations based in Vienna, has a well established track record for calling for "expanded diplomatic efforts," "dialogue and negotiation," and "mutual sincerity."[116] It is tactically astute for China to rhetorically support the IAEA

---

[115] Oster, Shai, "China plans to keep Iran oil projects moving ahead". Wall St. Journal, May 19, 2010.

[116] "China urges peaceful solution to Iranian nuclear issue." Xinhua, September 15, 2010

process, and to press Iran to provide greater cooperation, as these vague diplomatic niceties bolster China's credibility on the international stage but come at a very low strategic cost. At the end of the day China still holds the trump card: a Security Council veto. China has the luxury of positioning itself as a supportive and constructive member of the IAEA, knowing that before the most severe measures can be instituted, China will have the opportunity to weaken or veto UN sanctions, depending on the particular circumstances at that moment.

This in fact was the basic approach pursued by China during the previous U.S. presidential administration, in which the Bush foreign policy team worked hard on three occasions to secure Chinese support for a tougher stand on Iran, only to find the Chinese then turn around and work in the Security Council negotiating sessions to weaken those sanctions. This "push-pull" approach keeps the ball in the middle of the field and away from either team's goal, and achieves China's objective.

More recently, in April of this year, the Obama administration was able to win China's backing for tougher sanctions. However, as the price for its agreement, China was able to achieve a significant watering down in the sanctions, a carve-out for Chinese interests, and assurances of stable alternative supplies of oil in the event of any disruptions that would result if the Iranian situation ultimately boils over. More than a few seasoned observers sensed a certain déjà vu, harking back to the experience of the Bush Administration with China on the issue of sanctions.[117]

Setting aside the "headline grabbing" Iranian issue, and turning to the more mundane "working level," China has proven itself to be a dutiful and constructive institutional member of the IAEA. As has been seen in other organizations in which it participates, China has been proactive and effective in tapping into useful technical expertise possessed by the IAEA.

As part of its overall effort to secure sufficient energy supplies to fuel its continued economic growth, China has been aggressive in developing its nuclear power capacity, and it has shown a willingness to avail itself of the technical support that can be provided by the IAEA. For instance, in July 2010, at the request of the Chinese government an international team of 22 IAEA nuclear safety experts from 15 countries (including the United States) spent two weeks in China to review and provide recommendations on the nuclear safety regulatory environment in China.

The team visited "several nuclear facilities, including a nuclear power plant, a manufacturer of safety components for nuclear power plants, a research reactor, a fuel cycle facility, a waste management facility, industrial and medical radioactive sources and the nuclear and radiation accident emergency centre."[118]

There was a thorough review in a number of areas including "the government's responsibilities and

---

[117] Mcfarquar, Neil, "UN approves new sanctions to deter Iran". New York Times, June 9, 2010.

[118] "International nuclear safety experts conclude IAEA peer review of China's regulatory system", IAEA press release, July 30, 2010.

functions in the nuclear safety regime; the responsibilities and functions of the regulatory body and its management system; the activities of the regulatory body including authorizations; review and assessment; inspection and enforcement processes; and the development of regulations and guides."[119]

The team praised the cooperation of their Chinese counterparts, and provided extensive advice on further improving the nuclear safety system in China.

China has demonstrated seriousness in ensuring the security and safety of nuclear materials, and has constructively cooperated with the IAEA towards these ends. In August 2010, China and the IAEA signed an agreement to further increase their cooperation on nuclear safety and on the training and capacity building of nuclear safety personnel, and China has also joined the agency's Illicit Trafficking Database (ITDB) program.[120]

China has "worked" the IAEA system well, burnishing its international credentials and credibility, protecting and promoting its commercial and strategic interests, and obtaining valuable technical know-how.

Bank for International Settlements

Although China's role in the Bank for International Settlements (BIS) does not hold the same global impact as the other organizations under review, it is nonetheless an interesting case worth briefly surveying.

The most noteworthy aspect of China relationship with the BIS is that it provides an example of an organization in which China is actually somewhat "forward-leaning" as opposed to the defensive stance it assumes in so many other organizations.

The BIS administers the Basel Committee on Banking Supervision, which has grown in importance as a result of the Global Financial Crisis. The so-called Basel III framework which was announced last September constituted one of the most potentially important attempts to create an international regulatory response to the GFC. The center piece of the accord is a set of new, tougher standards on bank capital requirements, growing out of a recognition that one of the sparks of the crisis was over-leveraged banks. Basel III is intended to strengthen bank defense systems against a future financial catastrophe by requiring them to build up stronger buffers, including higher capital requirements.

---

[119] Ibid.

[120] "China reaffirms commitment to nuclear safety at IAEA meeting". Xinhua, September 14, 2010

To its critics, Basel III seems to be a rather meager approach, not the least of which is because it will be phased in gradually between now and 2019, leaving some to wonder: What happens in the meantime?

The Chinese approach has actually been interesting. For a variety of reasons, not the least of which are certain benefits which accrue to banks within a closed financial system, most of China's bank could meet the new Basel III capital requirements today.

China has been fairly "out in front" in attempting to push the envelope on Basel III. Liu Mingkang, the head of the China Banking Regulatory Commission has stated his view that the new Basel requirements are not enough when dealing with cross-border financial institutions. Instead, Liu expressed the view that "A more promising alternative is to introduce an international treaty, which sets fundamental rules for information-sharing, equal treatment of stakeholders across jurisdictions and depositor protection".[121]

One might expect to hear words like this from a European parliament politician in Brussels, rather than a leading Chinese government functionary, but nonetheless this is the official viewpoint of China's chief banking regulator. This is not the first or only time China has been forward-leaning with the Basel Committee. In 2008, China actually implemented the Basel II regulations ahead of schedule.[122]

China's conduct in the BIS/Basel Committee context demonstrates China's ability to be a constructive -- even enthusiastic – proponent of the international institutional structure, when those structures align tightly with the Chinese national interest.

---

[121] "The CBRC official briefs on the developments of the international reform of capital supervision." China Banking Regulatory Commission, September 17, 2010.

[122] Ma Wenluo, "China Implements Basel II Ahead of schedule", China Stakes, October 20, 2010 http://www.chinastakes.com/2008/10/china implements-basel-ii-ahead-of-schedule.html

Conclusions and Recommendations

The People's Republic of China approaches its participation in international organizations in much the same way as does the United States: it attempts to use these institutions as vehicles to advance its national geostrategic, economic, and political interests. Whether in international organizations or its bilateral or regional relationships, China is doing what great powers do: using hard and soft power to further solidify its positions.

As has been described throughout this report, what is most noteworthy is the sharp increase in China's **effectiveness** in using the international system to achieve its objectives, and the implications this holds for US interests, particularly on issues in which the US and Chinese national interest diverge.

Of perhaps greatest consequence, China's rising influence and increased effectiveness will impact the ability of the United States to pursue its interests within the international system, by constraining the ability of the United States to obtain "U.S. solutions."

A Diminished Capability to Apply "U.S. Solutions"

We are now emerging from an extended period in which the attractiveness of the U.S. model, combined with its financial wherewithal, and its geostrategic strength, has meant that the U.S. has frequently been able to secure -- and in some instances, impose -- "U.S. solutions" (i.e., solutions that overwhelmingly reflect US national interests and US philosophical foundations) on issues that are of a multilateral or even global nature.

In the 1980s, the United States was also confronted with a difficult currency issue involving the predominant Asian power, in that case Japan. The United States was able to corral Japan, along with the leading Western European economies, into agreeing to the U.S.-conceived policy approach: the so-called "Plaza Accord" of 1985, which engineered a significant appreciation in the Japanese yen vis-a-vis the U.S. dollar, a move that ultimately contributed to the U.S. success in pulling out of the recession of the early 1980s.

Although the Plaza Accord suited U.S. economic policy objectives at that time quite well, the impact on Japan was dubious at best, and some analysts have gone so far as to identify this "U.S. solution" as a contributing factor to Japan's subsequent "lost decade."

But today, as a result of China's rising influence and effectiveness on the world stage, this period of unrivaled ascendancy for "U.S. solutions" is now likely over. The capability of the United States to engineer and execute its vision of the preferred multilateral or bilateral policy approach to complicated global issues (currency or otherwise) is now significantly less than what it has been in recent decades.

To put it bluntly: There will be no "Plaza Accord" with China.

It has become unambiguously evident that Chinese monetary policy will be driven by an analysis of Chinese macroeconomic realities and domestic political imperatives. Foreign pressure, from the United States or elsewhere, has impacted these calculations only modestly, although the Chinese have proven adept at obtaining maximum "diplomatic mileage" out of economically minimalist adjustments they have made at politically opportune moments.

This pattern of well-timed symbolic gestures can be expected to continue (spurred on by the inflation-fighting benefits of a gradual appreciation). However, the type of fundamental change that most credible economists argue is necessary to address the imbalance – and certainly, anything on a par with the U.S.-driven 1985 Plaza Accord – is extremely unlikely.

China's success in shaping and even shifting the policies and positions of international institutions has further buttressed China's ability to resist U.S. pressure, and undermined the ability of the United States to secure "U.S. solutions." In subtle but increasing ways, international institutions are becoming more neutral or in some cases even supportive of the Chinese view on issues where the United States and China do not see eye to eye.

This is certainly the case on the exchange rate issue, for example, where China has successfully neutralized the G-20 by removing **any** reference (even positive) to China's currency valuation. This is also true in the IMF, where statements have taken on more of a "China will move at China's pace" tone, and harder hitting analysis done at the staff level is watered down by the time it reaches the political level, as in the case of the most recent Article IV consultations (see previous case study).

Solutions and policy approaches taken at the multilateral level will now increasingly reflect the interests and viewpoints not just of China, but also of a wider swath of nations, frequently but not always approximating the G-20. However, no other county in this wider constellation will wield anywhere near the power that China does. And while talk of a G-2 consisting of the United States and China, and holding predominant power, was greatly overstated and correctly discarded, <u>we are seeing the establishment of a different formulation that could be referred to as the **"G-2, plus 18."**</u>

In essence, this "G-2 plus 18" would be characterized by China's steadily growing ability to challenge and prevail over U.S. global economic orthodoxy (i.e., U.S. solutions) on the world stage. At the same time, a large number of other economically and strategically important countries (to varying degrees encouraged by the Chinese example) feel increasingly empowered to assert their views and project their national interests without necessarily falling into easy categorization of adhering to simplified notions of either a "Washington consensus" or a "Beijing consensus." And although none of these countries could hope in the near term to wield anywhere near the level of influence of the United States or China, on any given specific issue the impact of any of these countries could be profound. Policy makers in both Washington and Beijing would be well advised therefore to pay careful heed to the formation of a "Pretoria consensus," or "Brasilia consensus," or "Ankara consensus," or "New Delhi consensus."

In sum, *China's rapidly escalating effectiveness within the international system has spawned a significantly more complicated and multi-dimensional policy milieu for U.S. officials to navigate, and has decreased the capability of the United States to secure "first-choice" outcomes on multilateral policy issues.*

Importantly, China has grown increasingly comfortable and willing not merely to accumulate power, but to deploy its power more aggressively in support of its strategic interests. This reflects a growing confidence in its own capabilities and wherewithal, combined with a deepening perception that the ability of the United States to act as a counterweight to Chinese ambitions is on the wane. There has been, in effect, a sharp upward spike in the "real world" impact of China's power, as it is brought to bear in a greater number of settings and across a greater number of issues. This upward spike can be expected to continue, and sets the stage for what will likely be an increase in the frequency and intensity of disputes between the US and China on economic and strategic issues.

How can the US best cope with the implications of China's rising influence within the international system?

We offer the following recommendations:

1. Anticipate – and Prepare for -- a Period of "Probing"

Political leaders and policy makers in capitals from Brasilia to Beijing to Riyadh are now attempting to discern the extent to which we are in the opening stages of a tectonic plate shift in the established world economic and strategic order. Periodic rumblings of this plate shift had been felt with increasing frequency over the past 5-10 years, as China has continued its charge up the economic development ladder. The Global Financial Crisis provided the single biggest jolt to date.

It is however still too early to draw firm conclusions. Despite its growth, China also faces formidable challenges to its ability to maintain it trajectory. Growing incomes disparities, the threat of over-heating and/or the formation of massive asset bubbles, managing an unprecedented migration from rural to urban areas, and meeting the incredibly steep requirements for job growth, are all significant challenges that hold the potential to slow China's heretofore unimpeded ascent.

And the United States, despite the formidable challenges it faces, continues to be a highly innovative and resilient economy, and enjoys significant advantages as a result of the U.S. dollar status as the world's reserve currency. So although we are likely in some form of a transition phase, the exact parameters are unclear, and the precise impact of the "plate shift" is unknown. Just as in the immediate aftermath of a physical earthquake, no one is quite sure where the firm ground is, what has been destroyed, what is still standing, and how deep and strong the aftershocks will be.

During this phase, U.S. policy makers should anticipate a certain amount of "probing" from China (and also from middle powers such as Brazil and Turkey) as it tests the waters, and to seek to ascertain where, if anywhere, new boundaries or fault lines have been established. A crisis can be a golden opportunity for countries to carve out news roles and to seize, in a metaphorical sense, new territory. This process of testing and probing will frequently be played out in international institutions. U.S. policy-makers and representatives at international organizations should anticipate a period of "testing" and should be prepared to vigorously and aggressively push-back when U.S. strategic interests are involved during this probing process.

2. Accept the Inevitability of China's Rise

Within the U.S. policy community, there is a range of viewpoints on China's rising role and influence on the global stage in general, and in international organizations in particular. In some quarters of this community, China's rise is viewed with consternation, and even alarm. Move past this mindset. Setting aside the relative merits or demerits of this viewpoint, the simple fact of the matter is that China's increased relevance is reality. Although, as described above, the exact parameters are still unclear, we do know for certain that China is not "going anywhere." There is no plausible scenario that can be envisioned that would see China slide dramatically backwards.

Given this reality, there is broad recognition across the international community and in international institutions that China's rising economic power should and must be reflected in these organizations. It would be counter-productive for the United States to be seen, either in reality or perception, to be attempting to block this. And in any case, such an effort would ultimately be futile. Attempting to cling to institutional power structures that reflect the state of the world at the end of a war that ended 60 years ago would put the United States on the wrong side of history. It would also feed Chinese fears and insecurities that the United States is determined to "block" China, and likely would result in a hardening of Chinese positions.

3. Prepare for Greater Philosophical Competition

The United States has enjoyed an extended decades-long period in which its view of economic development, largely reflected in the Washington Consensus principles, was for the most part unchallenged within the leading international institutions. U.S. policy makers should anticipate and prepare for a period in which at least some tenants of these previously sacrosanct principles come under question. At the same time, a competing vision of economic development -- the so-called "Beijing consensus" -- is finding greater acceptance, especially in the developing world. This philosophical competition between differing views of development will necessarily seep into the international institutions in which both countries participate.

There has long been a school of thought in U.S. policy circles that stipulates that as countries progress up the economic development ladder, they will inevitably become more like the United States: in economic terms, a firm commitment to the wisdom of the marketplace, a light regulatory and government hand, and open trade and investment regimes; and in the political sphere, a more open, transparent, and democratic political system, fed by the wide open exchange of information fueled by the internet and other forms of modern telecommunications technology. For several decades, there was ample evidence to bear out this thesis. Today, however, we are seeing examples to suggest that this may no longer be the case.   For instance, the recent initial decision (although later modified) by the United Arab Emirates to restrict the use of Blackberries because of difficulties in conducting surveillance of encrypted messaging – as well as the interest of a number of other countries in following suit – suggest a new willingness to clamp down on information exchange, rather than moving inevitably towards greater openness.

Countries have been emboldened – partially by China's success and partially by the weaknesses that have been revealed in the U.S. approach – to pursue models, strategies, and policies that reflect differing national interests, cultural norms, political philosophies, and historical experiences, rather than simply and automatically following the U.S. path. Importantly, this does not suggest something as sweeping or simplistic as a swing of countries from the Washington Consensus to the Beijing Consensus. However, it does suggest a significant loosening of the grip of the Washington Consensus.

Strengthening relationships with key members of the "middle power" club is therefore essential. Indonesia, South Korea, Brazil, Vietnam, and Turkey are all countries to which the United States should pay more attention, both within and beyond the confines of the various international institutions in which they participate.

4. Relate to China in Terms it Understands

With all due apologies to James Carville: "It's the national interest, stupid." This slight modification of Carville's famous mantra from the 1992 presidential campaign provides a useful guidepost for understanding the motivation behind China's conduct within virtually all of the international organizations in which it participates. China's strategic and policy approach is driven by, and derived from, careful and studious consideration of Chinese national interests. Everything else is secondary – by far. Attempting to relate to, or to influence, China on any other basis is unlikely to yield any fruit. Appeals to China to act as a "responsible stakeholder" commensurate with its rising economic power are unlikely to impact Chinese policy calculations to any significant degree, and therefore should be dropped.

US trade officials have preached to their Chinese counterparts about the importance of intellectual property rights protection until they are blue in the face, but these efforts never produced the significant policy changes they sought. When did things slowly start to change and improve? When China began producing a level of home-grown innovation that requires greater IPR protection for the benefit of Chinese companies.

Israeli officials recently began making efforts to get China to play a greater and more constructive role on the issue of Iranian nuclear enrichment. Appeals were made to China's status as a rising power and its responsibility to helping ensure regional peace. All of these appeals received a polite hearing, but ultimately fell on deaf ears. The Chinese attitude markedly changed however when the Israeli officials opened up maps of shipping lanes and began describing the massive disruptions to the flow of Middle Eastern oil to China that would almost inevitably occur if the Israelis were to make a military strike on Iran, in the event that diplomatic means to resolve the stand-off were unsuccessful.[123]

Talk to the Chinese in a language they will understand and respond to.

Engage China is a frank "realpolitik" manner, and strike bargains when they make sense. Despite whatever differences might exist between the US and China, there is scope for cooperation. There are a range of issues on which common ground and common interests can be found.

5. Developed or Developing Country?

As China conducts its business in international intuitions, it sometimes presents two radically different faces, depending on circumstances. When it suits its purposes, China asserts itself as a leading economic super-power, second only to the US. And if we make judgments based on GDP figures, this is certainly correct. In fact, if the RMB were to be valued at the level that many economists believe reflects its fair value, the gap between the United States and China would be significantly tighter. However, this does not tell the whole story. If you consider per capita income, for example, China is much closer to El Salvador than it is to the United States – hardly an economic super-power. In a number of respects, and based on a number of economic criteria, China is still very much a developing country.

China has skillfully exploited this dichotomy, presenting itself as a humble voice from the developing world when that approach is advantageous, and in other instances, presenting itself as a leading economic power when that approach is suitable. U.S. policy makers should not let China have it both ways.

6. Anticipate Turbulence as We Approach 2012

The Hu Jintao/Wen Jiabao era of Chinese leadership is drawing to a close. Both Hu and Wen, along with a raft of other senior officials, are set to retire in 2012 or 2013. Although needless to say the Chinese political system differs markedly from that of the United States, there are similarities. One such similarity is the need for those who aspire to positions of power to shore-up their base and establish their credentials. In the Chinese context, this can oftentimes mean shoring up one's nationalistic credentials, and this is frequently epitomized by taking actions which are seen as "standing up" to the United States. Since international institutions provide a forum in which U.S. and Chinese interests are at

---

[123] Jacobs, Andrew. "Israel Makes Case to China for Iran Sanctions". New York Times, June 8, 2010.

play, policy makers should be prepared for the possibility of an increase in heated rhetoric and perhaps provocative actions as the inevitable jockeying for position takes place within the domestic Chinese political system in Beijing -- and the ripple effects radiate outwards to international organizations.

The upcoming Presidential election in Taiwan in 2012 could also stoke heated rhetoric as the notoriously messy Taiwanese electoral process plays out – with potential reverberations in the China-Taiwan-US triangle.

Be vigilant – the months leading up to 2012 could be politically fraught.

7. Be Pragmatic

Be pragmatic and flexible in assessing which institutions can best serve U.S. interests, and be open and willing to utilize alternative platforms to project U.S. interests when needed. Avoid a rigid adherence to institutional power structures that might have been relevant in previous decades, but which might be less so in the years and decades to come.

As a result of growing Chinese power and influence, the United States will find that China has a progressively stronger ability to block or deflect U.S. interests in international organizations in which the U.S. philosophy and viewpoint has historically dominated.

As any institution proves to be less conducive to U.S. objectives, the United States should look for other avenues to pursue its interests. For example, while the United States had to settle for weaker UN sanctions against Iran than it would have preferred in order to secure Chinese support, it opened a dialogue with the EU on a stronger batch of sanctions.   The Trans Pacific Partnership (TPP), a fledgling free trade area consisting of Australia, Brunei, Chile, New Zealand, Peru, Singapore, the United States, and Vietnam, also provides a useful example. [124]   While APEC's vision for a regional free trade area continues to be slow-tracked, the TPP allows a more ambitious sub-set of APEC members to try to advance the cause further on their own.   Importantly, this formulation keeps the United States in the center of the action, and undercuts the ability of China to establish ASEAN + 3 -- which excludes the United States -- as the region's preeminent platform for economic integration.   The TPP's ascension clause holds the possibility that this grouping could grow in size and economic importance.

Be pragmatic. When China's rising influence within a particular organization puts it in a position to deflect U.S. interests, look elsewhere.

---

[124] USTR Fact Sheet: Trans-Pacific Partnership. http://www.ustr.gov/about-us/press-office/fact-sheets/2009/november

CONCLUDING THOUGHT

A Final Point for Policy-makers to Ponder

While this study has been focused on the short and medium term, there is a critical longer term issue which U.S. policy makers will inevitably need to confront. In coping with China's growing influence in the international system, the U.S. approach thus far has been to offer China a greater accommodation within the system that the United States has established, but to keep the basic framework of that system in place, without any profound restructuring – and certainly without any alternations to the fundamental philosophical pillars upon which that system is built. Sixty long years after Bretton Woods, the international system is still largely fashioned in the U.S. image. The assumption that underlies the U.S. approach is that China will be content – or at least has no other choice – but to remain within the traditional U.S.-centric system as it is currently constituted.

This underlying assumption needs to be carefully reconsidered.

There are several realities that could render this assumption -- and the policy approaches based upon it -- false.

First and foremost, the question needs to be posed: Is it realistic to expect that China would be content playing a "game" that – from the Chinese perspective -- still appears tilted to the advantage of the United States and the West? Consider the governance of the IMF. While the United States has been supportive of the proposed realignment of voting rights within the IMF that would give a greater say to China and other developing countries, the actual impact and meaning of these increases is debatable due to the fact that the United States would continue to maintain its veto power (important decisions require 85%, and the US has a 17% vote), and at least for now, Europe continues to maintain its stranglehold on the top leadership position.

Although the West will try to make much of these reforms, the Chinese will correctly understand them as largely symbolic gestures. At some point, however, push will come to shove, and hard decisions will have to be made within any institution that wishes to remain relevant. With a finite number of seats at the table, countries like the Netherlands can no longer expect to play the same role they have in the past. Real -- rather than symbolic power -- will have to shift to China.

Another closely related factor is the increasing ability of China, acting either on a bilateral basis or through the establishment of new platforms and institutions, to supplant the "old guard" institutions – irrespective of whatever accommodations may or may not be made for China. As previously described, China's aid budget for Africa now exceeds that of the World Bank, so at least on the African continent the World Bank has arguably already been supplanted, and the nascent "Asian Monetary Fund" holds at least the potential to similarly challenge the relevance of the IMF. The West is trying to accommodate China by rearranging the deck chairs; the Chinese are building a new ship.

The full implications of these realities need to be carefully considered. China is a tactically shrewd and disciplined player who also happens to be in an exceedingly strong position. China can simultaneously push for, obtain, and exercise, increased power within the existing system, while at the same time establishing and promoting alternative vehicles that exclude the United States, and are more conducive to China's interests.

We are still in the opening moves of what is likely to be a protracted chess match. Nothing should be assumed or taken for granted. But at a minimum, U.S. policy makers need to consider at least the possibility that over the longer term: 1) China will no longer need to be content operating strictly within the confines of a U.S.-led system, and will be in a position to shift power to alternative institutions; and 2) China, by dint of its growing economic and strategic power, could eventually be in a position to fundamentally alter the existing system in ways far beyond the largely token reforms currently under consideration.

A clear, long-term policy approach to cope with these possibilities needs to be discussed, debated, and developed -- now.

Bibliography

Abdoulaye Wade, Senegal's President, "Time for the west to practice what it preaches", Financial Times, Jan 23, 2008, http;//www.ft.com/cms/s/5d347f88-c897-11dc-94a6-0000779fd2ac,dwp_uuid=8735dcb2

"ADB , Bank of China to Broaden Strategic Cooperation." Asian Development Bank, Jul y 13, 2010 http://www.adb.org/Media/printer.asp?articleID=13278

Allan Beattie, "IMF in discord over renminbi", Financial Times, January 26, 2010, http://www.ft.com/cms/s/b876fafc-eb18-11dd-bb6e-0000779fd2ac

Alan Wheatley, "I.M.F. turns on the charm in Asia", Business With Reuters, July 22, 2010

Alexander Casella, "Macedonia: Taiwan's Lost Gambit", *Asia Times Online*, July 11, 2001.

Alden, Chris. "China and Africa's Natural Resources: The Challenges and Implications for Development and Governance." September 2009, South African Institute of International Affairs.

"A look at Chinese peacekeepers' daily mission in Haiti", Xinhua news, January 21 2010 http://news.xinhuanet,com/english2010/china/2010-01/22/c_13147038.htm

Andrew Scheineson, "The Shanghai Cooperation Organization", March 24, 2009, http://www.c fr.org/publication/10883/shanghai_cooperation_organization.html

Andrew F. Cooper and Thomas Fues, "Do the Asian Drivers Pull Their Diplomatic Weight? China, India, and The United Nations", *World Development*, Vol. 36, No. 2, 2008

Antoaneta Bezlova, "Kosovo Holds Lesson for Tibet, Taiwan", Inter Press Service (IPS) News Agency, February 19, 2008.

Antoaneta Bezlova, "Lin Yifu's World Bank Job May Add to China's Clout", http://ipsnews.net/print.asp?idnews=41010

Articles of Agreement of the International Monetary Fund, http://www.imf.org/external/pubs/ft/aa/index.htm

"Asian Development Bank : Overview of Support to China", Asian Development Bank 2010

Bates Gill and Chin-Hao Huang, "China spreads its peacekeepers", Asia Times Online, February 4, 2009.

Beattie, Alan, and James Politi. "US Welcomes Loosening of Renmimbi Peg." Financial Times, July 9, 2010 http://www.ft.com/cms/s/0/4250604c-8af0-11df-bead-00144feab49a.html

Bezlova, Antoaneta. "Lin Yifu's World Bank Job May Add To China's Clout." Inter Press Service. January 31, 2008, http://ipsnews.net/print.asp?idnews=41010

Brown, Kevin. "Biggest Regional Trade Deal Unveiled", Financial Times, January 1, 2010.

"China and Taiwan: The Ties that Bind?" The Economist.,July 3, 2010.

"China and the I.M.F." The New York Times, 8 Aug 010, http://nytimes.com/2010/08/09/opinion /09mon2.html?_r.html 4a.China and The G20 China Takes The Centre Stage" The Economist. 31 Mar 2009 <http://en.ccer.edu.cn/ReadNews.asp?NewsID=6656

China Banking Regulatory Commission, The CBRC official briefs on the developments of the international reform of capital supervision,   September 17, 2010 http;//www.cbrc.gov.cn/English/home/jsp/docView.jsp?docID=201010127105895E82201

"China Confirms Deaths of all 8 Chinese Police Officers in Haiti Quake". Xinhua, January 17, 2010.

"China rolls out assistance blueprint for ASEAN", Xinhua, April 24, 2009, http://news.xinhuan

"Chinese participation in APEC Significant: Minister", People's Daily Online, http://english.peopledaily.com.cn/english/200110/16/print20011016_82414.html

"15th Chinese Peacekeeping Force deploys in East Timor for rotation duty", People's Daily, May 12, 2010.

"Chinese Peacekeeping reinforcements arrive in Haiti", Xinhua News Agency, January 26, 2010.

"Chinese professor named World Bank chief economist", Washington (AFP), February 4, 2008, http: //afp.google.com/article/ALeqM5h-J1IKQZ_r-4SukILjHli-BvFxZw

"China plays down impact of Basel III on local banks" The Economic Times, October 14,2010 http://economictimes.indiatimes.com/articleshow/6573512.cms?prtpage=1

"China Policy: Yuanimpressed." The Economist, July 3, 2010: 33-34.

"China Pledges More Military Aid to Cambodia." Asian Political News, May 3, 2010 http://findarticles.com/p/articles/mi_m0WDQ/is_2010_May_3/ai_n53397127/?tag=content;col1.6.

"China Slams ADB Over India Funding." Sina.com. June 19, 2009 http://english.sina.com/china/2009/0618/249531.html. 7.

"China ups Lebanon force to 1,000", BBC News, September 18, 2006.

"China urges peaceful solution to Iranian nuclear issue." Xinhua, September 15, 2010

"China Vows New Food Safety Campaign", Xinhua, October 2, 2010.

"China watchdog says Basel III not enough, calls for treaty", Reuters, October 7, 2010 http://www.reuters.com/assets/print?aid=USTOE696070201010107

"Copenhagen Accord of 18 December 2009". Http://unfccc.int

Davis, Bob. "US Presses China on Currency", Wall Street Journal, July 9, 2010.

"Declaration on the Conduct of Parties in the South China Sea", ASEAN, 2002.

Dingmin, Zhang. "IMF Names Zhu Min as Adviser, Showing China's Clout (Update 1)." Bloomberg Businessweek. February 24, 2010, http://www.businessweek.com/news/2010-02-24/imf-names-zhu-as-adviser-showing-china-s-increasing-influence.html .

Documents of the Twelfth National Congress of the Communist Party of China, Joint Publishing Company Ltd, Hong Kong, 1982.

"End to World Bank's Chad Oil Deal." BBC News, September 10, 2008, http://news.bbc.co.uk/go/pr/fr/-/2/hi/business/7608163.stm.

"First echelon of 7th Chinese peacekeeping force to Sudan sets out", People's Liberation Army Daily, July 19, 2010.

Foroohar, Rana, and Melinda Liu. "It's China's World We're Just Living In It." Newsweek, Mach 12, 2010 http://www.newsweek.com/id/234928/output/print

"G20 Drops China Sensitive Plaudits on Yuan Reform." Reuters, June 2010.

Garnaut, John. "Don't Push US, China Warns Rich Countries". Sydney Morning Herald, January 11, 2010.

Geoff Dyer, "Beijing 'steals US thunder' ahead of G20", Financial Times, June 20, 2010.

Geoff Dyer, "G20 Looks to Beijing to Drive Global Growth", Financial Times, July 11, 2010

Greenlees, Donald, "The Search for a New Financial Order", Global Asia, December 2008

Halper, Stefan. The Beijing Consensus: How China's Authoritarian Model Will Dominate The Twenty-First Century. New York: Basic Books, 2010.

Huang, Yiping. "China's New Policy Strategy and The G20." East Asia Forum. March 29, 2009 http://www.eastasiaforum.org/2009/03/29/g20-chinas-new-policy-strategy/print/

Hoyos, Carola. "China Now World's Biggest Energy User." Financial Times. July 19, 2010 http://www.ft.com/cms/s/0/937fdd2c-934b-11df-bb9a-00144feab49a.html

Ian Taylor, "The Two Chinese Compete in Africa", Contemporary Review, October 1997.

"IMF and World Bank Meetings Show China's Rising Influence: Backgrounder: Timeline of Developing Countries Rise In the IMF." People's Daily Online, April 27, 2010 http://english.peopledaily.com.cn/90001/90778/90862/6964851.html

IMF Executive Board Concludes 2010 Article IV Consultation with China, Public Information Notice (PIN) No. 10/100, 27 July 2010.

International Crisis Group, "China's Growing Role in UN Peacekeeping", Asia Report No. 166, April 17, 2009.

"International nuclear safety experts conclude IAEA peer review of China's regulatory system", IAEA press release, July 30, 2010.

Jacobs, Andrew. "Israel Makes Case to China for Iran Sanctions". New York Times, June 8, 2010.

Jacques, Martin. "Chinese in Top Job at World Bank". China Daily, March 6, 2008

Jacques, Martin. "The Citadel of The Global Economy Are Yielding to China's Battering Ram." The Guardian. 23 Apr 2008, http://www.guardian.co.uk/commentisfree/2008/apr/23/imf.china.print

Jacques, Martin. When China Rules The World: The Rise of The Middle Kingdom and The End of The Western World. London: Penguin Group, 2009.

Jonathan D. Ostry, Atish R.Gosh, Karl Habermeier, Marcos Chamen, Mahuash S . Quresh, and Dennis B.S. Reinhardt, "Capital Inflows: The Role of Controls, http://www.imf.org/external/pubs/ft/spn/2010/spn1004.pdf

Lamont, James. "ADB Adopts Piecemeal Strategy In India After Chinese Objections." Financial Times. 28 November 28, 2009 , http://www.ft.com/cms/s/0/57d88396-dbbd-11de-9424-00144feabdc0.html

Lee, Peter. "China Discovers Value In the IMF." A Times.com, June 10, 2009, http://www.atimes.com/atimes/China_Business/KF10Cb01.html

Ling, 1997.

MacKinnon, Mark. "What China Wants From The G20." Globe and Mail, June 7, 2010 http://www.theglobeandmail.com/news/world/g8-g20/economy/what-china-wants-from-the-g20/article1595426/

Major General Zhang Qinsheng, interview with Xinhua News Agency, September 28, 2006, as quoted in Bonny Ling, " China's Peacekeeping Diplomacy", China Rights Forum, Human Rights in China, No. 1, 2007.

Mark Lynas, "How do I know China wrecked the Copenhagen deal? I was in the room", guardian.co.uk, December 22, 2009, http;//www.guardian.co.uk/environment/2009/dec/22/copenhagen-climate-change-mark.

Mark Weisbrot,"Standing up to the I.M.F", International Herald Tribune, October 7 2010.

Martin Jacques, "Chinese in top job at World Bank", Chinadaily, June 3, 2008, http://www.chinadaily.com.cn/business/2008-06/03/content_6731511.htm

Ma Wenluo, "China Implements Basel II Ahead of schedule", China Stakes, October 20, 2010 http://www.chinastakes.com/2008/10/china implements-basel-ii-ahead-of-schedule.html

Mcfarquar, Neil, "UN approves new sanctions to deter Iran". New York Times, June 9, 2010

Minder, Raphael. "China Blocks ADB India Loan Plan." Financial Times. April 10, 2009 http://www.ft.com/cms/s/0/033935c2-25e4-11de-be57-00144feabdc0.html

Ministry of Foreign Affairs, Republic of China (Taiwan), "Diplomatic Allies", http://www.moga.gov.tw/webapp/ct.asp?xltem=32618&CtNode=1379&mp=6

Nye, Joseph. Soft Power: The Means to Success in World Politics. New York: Public Affairs, 2004.

"Not Exactly Eye To Eye." The Economist. May 29, 2010: 31-32.

Oster, Shai, "China plans to keep Iran oil projects moving ahead". Wall St. Journal, May 19, 2010.

Ostry, Jonathan D. ,et al . "Capital Inflows: The Role of Controls." International Monetary Fund. February 19, 2010, http://www.imf.org/external/pubs/ft/spn/2010/spn1004.pdf

P. Parameswaran, "The financial crisis and Asian connections, October 20, 2010 http://blogs.afp.com/?post/2008/10/20/The-financial-crisis-and-Asian-connections

Patten, Chris. "Is China Hiding Its Brightness and Biding Its Time?" The National. February 24, 2010 http://www.thenational.ae/apps/pbcs.dll/article?AID=/20100225/OPINION/702249853&SearchID=7339 8228100549

Peter Browne, "China's Copenhagen Paradoxs", Inside Story, January 14, 2010, http://inside.org.au/chinas-copenhagen-paradox/

"Position Paper of the People's Republic of China on the United Nations Reforms", Beijing, June 7, 2005, quoted in Ramesh Thakur, The United Nations, Peace and Security, Cambridge University Press, 2006.

Prestowitz, Clyde V., The betrayal of American prosperity : free market delusions, America's decline, and how we must compete in the post-dollar era. New York: Free Press, 2010.

Prestowitz, Clyde V., Three Billion New Capitalists - The Great Shift of Wealth and Power to the East. New York: Basic Books, 2005. 25 Robin Harding, "IMF staff and board split on renminbi", Financial Times, July 28, 2010, http://www.ft.com/cms/s/446e983c-9a70-11df-87fd-00144feab49a,dwp_uuid=f6e7043e-6d

Samantha, Pranab Dhal. "China Says No but US, Japan help ADB clear India's Plan." Indian Express.com. June 16, 2009, http://www.indianexpress.com/story-print/477252/

State of The Region 2009 – 2010. The Pacific Economic Cooperation Council (PECC), 2009.

Statement by Dr. ZHOU Xiaochuan Governor of the People's Bank of China at the Twenty-First Meeting of the International Monetary and Financial Committee Washington D.C., April 24, 2010 http://www.cbrc.gov.cn/english/home/jsp/docView.jsp?docID=201010127105895E82201

Statement by H.E. Ambassador LIU Zhenmin at the Open Debate of the Security Council on 'Protection of Civillians in Armed Conflicts", Permanent Mission of the People's Republic of China to the UN, November 20, 2007.

Strauss-Kahn, Dominique. "Asia and the Global Economy: Leading the Way Forward in the 21st Century." International Monetary Fund, July 12,2010 http://www.imf.org/external/np/speeches/2010/071210.htm

"The CBRC official briefs on the developments of the international reform of capital supervision." China Banking Regulatory Commission, September 17, 2010.

The G-20 Toronto Summit Declaration, June 26-27, 2010

United Nations Department of Peacekeeping Operations, Fact Sheet, "United Nations Peacekeeping", March, 2010.

United Nations, Meeting Record, S/PV.2313, December 14, 1981.

United Nations Mission for the Referendum in Western Sahara (MINURSO), "Press release", Laayoune, September 17, 2007.

"UN official lauds China's peacekeeping efforts" Xinhua News Agency, July 30, 2010.

United Nation Press Release, "Chinese company of engineers arrives in Sudan to support joint United Nations-African Union mission in South Darfur", July 18, 2008.

United Nation Security Council, "Security Council Fails to Adopt Draft Resolution on Myanmar, Owing to Negative Votes by China, Russian Federation", January 12, 2007, and "China says Burma crisis should be resolved by dialogue", Kyodo News, October 25, 2007.

United Nations Security Council, Resolution 1674, April 28, 2006.

"U.S Cuts Military Aid to Cambodia for Deporting Uyghurs to China." Asian Political News, April 5, 2010 http://findarticles.com/p/articles/mi_m0WDQ/is_2010_April_5/ai_n53035608/?tag=content;col1

USTR Fact Sheet: Trans-Pacific Partnership. http://www.ustr.gov/about-us/press-office/fact-sheets/2009/november

Wade, Abdoulaye. "Time For The West to Practise What It Preaches." Financial Times. January 23, 2008 http://www.ft.com/cms/s/0/5d347f88-c897-11dc-94a6-0000779fd2ac.html

Ward, Andrew. "China At The G20 Meeting in Toronto." Economic Observer News, June 29, 2010 http://www.eeo.com.cn/ens/homepage/briefs/2010/06/29/174089.shtml

Wheatley, Alan. "A Year After Lehman, Assertive China Eyes Influence." Reuters, September 15,2009 http://www.reuters.com/assets/print?aid=USTRE58D39220090915

Wheatley, Alan. " I.M.F. turns on the charm in Asia" Reuters, July 20, 2010.

Wolf, Martin. "Wheel of Fortune Turns as China Outdoes West." Financial Times, September 14, 2009.

Wolverson, Roya. "Confronting The China – U.S. Economic Imbalance." Council On Foreign Relations. February 17, 2010, http://www.cfr.org/publication/20758/confronting_the_chinaus_economic_imbalance.html

Xiaochuan, Zhou. "Reform the International Monetary System." The People's Bank of China, March 23, 2009, http://www.pbc.gov.cn/english/detail.asp?col=6500&ID=178

Xin, Zhou and Chris Buckley. "China Wants Support on IMF Voting at G20." Reuters, September 15, 2009 http://www.reuters.com/assets/print?aid=USTRE58E29D20090915

Xinhua. "China to Boost Ties with Chad, Says Senior Chinese Official." People's Daily Online. 24 October 24, 2008, http://english.people.com.cn/90001/90776/90883/6521088.html

Xinhua, "Chinese vice premier orders more efforts to improve food savety", April 19, 2010,http://news.xinhuanet.com/english2010/china/2010-04/20/c_13258667.htm

Yin He, "The peacekeeping dragon is on safari", Asia Times Online, February 8, 2008, and "Timor police to carry guns", BBC News, February 10, 2000.

Zakaria, Fareed. The Post- American World. New York: W.W Norton & Company, 2008.

Zoellick, Robert. "Whither China: From Membership to Responsibility" Speech, September 21, 2005.